Firestone Books
Success Begins Here

English Language Revision Guide for GCSE

This guide is also dyslexia-friendly!

Jane Hallwood

Series Editor: Nicola Walsh

This no-nonsense guide has all you need to do brilliantly at your English Language GCSE

firestonebooks.com

English Language Revision Guide for GCSE
Dyslexia-Friendly Edition
Jane Hallwood

This dyslexia-friendly edition has a large easy-to-read font, minimal italics and capital letters, large line spacing, and is printed on cream paper – all combining to ensure an easier reading experience.

Series Editor: Nicola Walsh

Cover © XL Book Cover Design
xlbookcoverdesign.co.uk

2021 Edition

ISBN-13: 9781909608450

Published by Firestone Books

firestonebooks.com

You can stay up to date by following Firestone Books on Facebook and Twitter, or subscribing to our fabulous newsletter.

~ Contents ~

About this guide   5
About the key skills   6

Section 1: Reading skills

Reading for meaning   10
Writers' choices about language   23
Writers' choices about structure   50
Making critical comparisons   71
Making a personal critical response to texts   96

Section 2: Writing skills

Quality of language   114
Writing articles   119
Writing letters   124
Writing speeches   132
Development, structure and organisation   138
Expanding your ideas   149
Technical accuracy: sentence structures for effect   156
Technical accuracy: punctuation for effect   163

Some final words   168

Reading texts

Text A   170
Text B   173
Text C   176

Our fabulous new books are out now!

Revision Guides for GCSE

- Jekyll and Hyde
- An Inspector Calls
- Macbeth

25 Key Quotations for GCSE

- Romeo and Juliet
- A Christmas Carol
- Macbeth
- Jekyll and Hyde
- An Inspector Calls

But if you can't wait to get your hands on some of our books, we've got a host of annotation-friendly editions, containing oodles of space for you to fill with those all-important notes:

Annotation-Friendly Editions

- Jekyll and Hyde
- An Inspector Calls
- A Christmas Carol
- Romeo and Juliet
- Macbeth
… and lots more!

And that's not all - we've got **all** these books available in super-helpful **dyslexia-friendly** and **large print** editions too!

Available through Amazon, Waterstones, and all good bookshops!

~ About this guide ~

This guide has been designed to provide you with everything you need to help you gain your best grade in English. It covers the key skills for GCSE English Language for all grades and exam boards. The guide aims to provide you with a deeper understanding of essential key skills. In order to help you with that, the guide provides you with many examples and explanations. It is based around three texts which are reproduced at the end of the guide. It's a good idea to read them through and familiarise yourself with them before you start.

You will find that each unit covers the full spectrum of responses, explaining how to progress within each key skill. You may focus on the top responses if you want. However, it's always helpful to understand what the simplest responses are like, even if that's just to avoid making the same mistakes. It will help you to understand how progress is built on in each of these key elements. It will particularly help you if you are stuck at a particular mark on one question in order to help you understand the concepts that will help you progress.

~ About the key skills ~

Key skills underpin everything at GCSE. Whilst these vary slightly in how they are assessed across exam boards, you will find all of these skills assessed at some point.

Reading for meaning

What this means:

a) Summarise.

b) Bring together and synthesise evidence.

c) Identify explicit and implicit information and ideas.

d) Evaluate the usefulness of what you read.

e) Seek evidence to support a point of view.

f) Make comparisons.

Skimming, **scanning** and **close reading** skills will be useful to help you **find information** and **find connections and contrasts**. These reading skills are used for different purposes, either working quickly across a text or texts, or reading in depth. Reading for meaning also involves making judgements about the usefulness of the evidence you find, as well as evaluating the ideas the writers express.

Writers' choices with language and structure

What this means:

a) Analyse how writers use language.

b) Explore how writers use structure.

c) Explore how writers create effects and influence readers.

d) Use relevant subject terminology to support your views.

e) Evaluate the effects of writers' choices.

This means **identifying the techniques the writer is using**, then discussing the meaning, ideas or viewpoint they convey as well as considering the writer's purpose. You will need to **understand how language features and structural devices work** to create meaning.

Making critical comparisons

What this means:

    a) Find evidence from two texts.

    b) Compare writers' ideas, views and perspectives across two texts.

    c) Compare writers' techniques and styles across two texts.

What is being tested here is whether or not you can find the similarities or the differences between two texts as well as **understanding how** writers shared their views with us as readers. It builds on your ability to **find key evidence** and your ability to **understand how writers use language features and structural devices** to create meaning.

Making a critical personal response to reading

What this means:

    a) Evaluate a text critically.

    b) Form your own opinions about a text.

    c) Support your evaluation with evidence from the text.

    d) Explore alternative views.

Evaluating a text critically means **explaining what you think and why**. It is also testing other key skills, such as your ability to **find evidence** from a text, and your **understanding of how writers use language features and structural devices** to create more subtle meanings. You are asked to write at length in these questions which are always worth the most marks on the comprehension section.

Writing skills

What this means:

a) Communicate clearly, effectively and imaginatively.

b) Adapt your writing for purpose and audience.

c) Write to narrate, describe or give your opinion.

d) Write in different forms.

e) Organise information and ideas.

f) Use a variety of different structures for your writing.

g) Use vocabulary and linguistic devices for effect.

h) Use grammatical and structural features to link your ideas together.

What you are being tested on is your ability to **create content** and **organise your ideas** for different types of writing, including narrative and non-narrative writing, chronological and non-chronological writing, and fiction and non-fiction writing.

The **audience, purpose and form** will change in each exam, so you need to be prepared to write a range of **text types** and to choose your **formality** appropriately. The **purpose** can also change. You could be asked to narrate, describe, explain, instruct, advise, argue or persuade. That means you'll need to understand the different ways to express your ideas for each of these purposes. There are a number of **forms** that you could be asked to write in: articles, letters, speeches, leaflets and essays.

Technical accuracy

What this means:

a) Use a range of vocabulary and sentence structures for clarity, purpose and effect.

b) Use accurate spelling and punctuation.

What you're being tested on here is your ability to **write clearly**. You're also being tested on your ability to **use technical aspects of writing for effect**, to influence or engage the reader.

How answers are graded in this book

Answers are not graded. There are no 'Grade 9' or 'Grade 1' answers in this book. Instead, you will find answers that are:

- **Basic** (limited, incorrect or brief).
- **Straightforward** (attempted, inconsistent, uneven or undeveloped).
- **Successful** (appropriate, clear, accurate or relevant).
- **Skilled** (perceptive, developed, full, detailed, explanatory or analytical).

That said, if you are working for Grade 3, you should be aiming for **straightforward answers**. If you are working for Grade 5, you should be aiming for **successful answers**, and if you are aiming for Grade 8 or above, you should be aiming for **skilled answers**.

Understanding what these skills look like and how to progress within them is the core of this guide.

Section 1: Reading skills

~ Reading for meaning ~

What you are being tested on

- Can you **find details** from the text?
- Can you **identify** information?
- Can you handle **two different texts** and **synthesise** the information that you find?

Your exam paper may reproduce the text separately on an insert or a resource book. They may alternatively include it as part of the question paper. You will need to annotate, underline and highlight this text as you skim, scan, compare or close read.

Many of your questions for GCSE English relate to **specific and different** parts of the passage. If you are selecting details from the wrong part of the passage, you won't be able to gain marks. If you are given specific lines in the question, **mark off the lines** to avoid referring to the wrong sections. Put a box around them as a visual reminder.

Close reading

Close reading means studying a small part of the text to **find precise words, facts or details**. Often the question will ask you to focus on a given part of the text which is where you will use your close reading skills.

When we use close reading skills, we need to read all the words in a short section of the text. You can also use **text-marking**, **underlining** or **highlighting** to **identify key words**.

In order to improve your close reading skills, you will be focusing on a short extract at the beginning of Text C from page 176. This extract is taken from the middle of a short story by HG Wells. The narrator is about to spend a night in a haunted room. You will be practising your close reading skills on this brief section.

The section is reprinted below.

The door to the red room and the steps up to it were in a shadowy corner. I moved my candle from side to side, in order to see clearly before opening the door and I had a sudden twinge of apprehension. I glanced over my shoulder, and opened the door rather hastily, with my face half turned to the silence of the landing.

I entered, closed the door behind me at once, turned the key I found in the lock, and stood with the candle held up surveying the scene, the great red room of Lorraine Castle in which the young duke had died.

Sample task

Read lines 1-10 of Text C.

List **four** things you learn about the narrator in these lines

Understanding how you are marked

You will be marked on how many correct responses you make. Here are some of the things you might have said about the narrator:

He was at the bottom of some steps, was in front of a door, had a candle, moved the candle from side to side, wanted to see clearly, opened the door, felt a sudden twinge of apprehension, glanced over his shoulder, opened the door rather hastily, entered the room, closed the door behind him, locked the door, surveyed the scene, was in the great red room, was in Lorraine Castle.

How to improve your answer

In questions like this which assess your close reading skills, you are often being tested on your ability to **find information** in a **given part of the extract.** So if it says lines 1 to 8 then any detail from anywhere else may be perfectly right, but won't be marked.

To check your answer, ask: **'Is it from the right lines?'**

After telling you where to look, the question will tell you how many things you are expected to find: 'List **five** things you learn about' or 'Identify **a word** or **phrase**'.

Then it tells you the **subject of the question**.

In this example, it is the narrator.

The subject is vital. It helps you frame your answer. Make sure you are answering the actual question, not the question you think you've been asked. **Write the subject at the beginning of your response** for example:

1. **The narrator** had a candle.
2. **The narrator** opened the door.

And so on.

This stops you writing about things that are off the subject. Ask yourself: **'Is it about the subject?'**

Finally, ask yourself: **'is it true?'**

This can be tricky.

This question is easy for teachers to mark when students copy exactly from the passage, changing words slightly to make sense, changing 'I' to 'he' and so on. But it becomes a nightmare when students try to make inferences or discuss what things mean. If you are asked for a quote and you give an inference, you won't gain marks on this type of question. There are many students who feel that this question is easy and they should make it harder for themselves, then making it impossible to get the marks.

Copying out is perfectly acceptable; for some exam boards, it's the only way you will get marks if asked to **find** or **copy out**. You don't need to make inferences to get the marks. Unless it asks you to explain, if you are asked to **find** information, do exactly as you are asked.

1. **Look at the question first** and **underline the key words of the question**.
2. **Mark off the lines** you are asked to find your answers from.
3. **Read every word** in those lines carefully and **highlight possible answers**.

The door to the red room and the steps up to it were in a shadowy corner. I moved my candle from side to side, in order to see clearly before opening the door and I had a sudden twinge of apprehension. I glanced over my shoulder, and opened the door rather hastily, with my face half turned to the silence of the landing.

I entered, closed the door behind me at once, turned the key I found in the lock, and stood with the candle held up surveying the scene, the great red room of Lorraine Castle in which the young duke had died.

4. Start your answer by **copying out the subject of the question** or using a pronoun if the question demands it. For example, 'The narrator' and then 'he/she'.

5. **Copy out a relevant detail** from the right lines.

6. **Check it makes sense**.

7. Check: Is it from the right lines? Is it about the subject? Is it true?

8. Check: Have I got as many pieces of evidence as there are marks or that I have been asked to find?

9. Check whether you need to copy a direct quotation or whether you can make an inference.

Example responses and commentary

1 mark

1. The narrator was spending the night in a haunted room ✗

2. The narrator wanted to prove there is nothing to be scared of ✗

3. The narrator was in Lorraine Castle ✔

4. The narrator was terrified ✗

The answers on lines 1 and 2 are not in the given lines even though they are correct. The answer on line 4 may be about a 'sudden twinge of apprehension' but feeling apprehensive or a little scared is not the same as feeling terrified. It is not true. Always check where you are taking your answers from.

2 marks

1. In a shadowy corner ✘
2. Opened the door ✔
3. Turned to the silence of the landing ✘
4. Locked the door ✔

Although the student might mean that the narrator is in a shadowy corner, the text says the 'steps' are in a shadowy corner. It's impossible to tell whether the student thought the steps and/or the narrator was in the shadowy corner. It's impossible to guess what the person who wrote this answer meant. Always put in the subject of the question. Make sure you copy out the phrase correctly and entirely.

3 marks

1. The narrator moved from side to side ✘
2. The narrator had a sudden twinge of apprehension ✔
3. He glanced over his shoulder ✔
4. He was in a room where someone had died ✔

The answer on the first line is wrong as it is not true: it was the candle that moved from side to side. Always check that what you write is about the subject of the question.

4 marks

1. The narrator opened the door to the red room ✔

2. The narrator was in Lorraine Castle ✔

3. The narrator had a candle ✔

4. The narrator had a sudden twinge of apprehension ✔

They're all from the right lines. They're all about the narrator. They're all true.

Summary

- Read the question first and underline key words.
- Make sure you stick to the right lines by putting a box around them.
- Use the words of the question to start off your answer.
- If you are asked to identify a word or phrase, make sure you quote directly.
- If you put the text into your own words, make sure you are careful that it makes sense. Also, make sure this is acceptable if you are asked to find details rather than explain.

Other questions will give you a brief statement and ask you to use your close reading skills to find a quote that matches it. For instance, it may say:

> **Read lines 1-8 of Text C.**
>
> Find **one detail** that suggests the writer is nervous.

You may also find other questions that do a similar thing, giving you a statement to match to evidence. You may also be asked to decide whether an inference that you are given as part of the question is true or false.

Scanning

Other questions will require you to find evidence from a much broader section of text. On questions where you are asked to find selected information from the whole text but on a very narrow focus or subject, or questions where you are asked to handle two texts to find points of comparison, you can find yourself with almost two thousand words to sift through for a very small number of precise points and marks.

For this task you will be referring to non-fiction Text A and Text B on page 170 - 173 of this guide.

Sample task

To answer the following question you must use both texts.

Both texts describe the people that the writers worked with when younger.

What similarities do the other workers share in these texts in the way that they behave?

Understanding how you are marked

The mark scheme is divided into three:

1. Your use of **references relating to a specific focus.**
2. Your ability to pick out **points of comparison or contrast** across two texts.
3. Your ability to **infer meaning** from both texts.

The question also gives you a very narrow, specific subject to focus on, and if you want to do well on this question, you will need to **refer only to that subject**. You will have two texts to scan through once you have identified this focus. You're being tested to see if you can handle a whole text or more, rather than one small section, such as the close reading questions.

How to improve your answer

When scanning, good readers use a number of techniques to help them. The best way to scan is with a highlighter. You're going to focus on one very narrow key idea.

Go to the question and **underline or highlight key words**.

> To answer the following question you must use both texts.
>
> Both texts describe **the people that the writers worked with when younger**.
>
> What **similarities** do the **other workers share** in these texts **in the way that they behave**?

That gives you the key focus for your scanning: things the other workers <u>do</u>.

Once you have identified the key focus, **scan with a highlighter**. Work through the text systematically at speed. You don't have to read every word. **Search for the key words**, then when you find them, **read around the key word** to find more details.

Simpler questions will only ask you to scan through one text and find information relating to that one text. For instance, you could find this on questions relating to the structure of the whole passage. You will also be using your scanning skills on longer essay-style questions as well as on questions asking you to compare the views and perspectives in two different passages.

Where you are asked to find details from two sources, **make a long selection first** and then **narrow down**.

> Other than John, the milkman, it was a world of adolescents. He stayed mostly in the float driving, and we hung off the back or ran to catch up. There were usually three of us most mornings and we'd spend most of our time chatting. We'd hang out on Friday and Saturday nights too. It turns out deep friendships are forged in those ice-cold winter mornings.

- Include everything you think *might* be relevant at this point.
- Then do the same for the second text.
- After that, look through the parts you highlighted and narrow down your focus.

Then **check your choices against the question**, focusing on the quotes that are very clearly about the key words in the question. In this case, it is what the other workers do.

Here, a student has compiled a list of all the details that they found that they thought were focused on the key words of the question:

Focused details from Text A	Focused details from Text B
He stayed mostly in the float driving	Some of the other workers have broken their hands or feet stopping the spindles moving.
Anne and Margaret ... ran the shop like a comedy act ... sharp humour and acid tones.	If you were a boy or a girl, they gave you the strap if you were slow.
Everybody had their role and the shop ran smoothly, except when the boss turned up.	Sometimes the overlooker is so angry with us he'll take one of the girls and beat her the full length of the room with a chain or with the strap.
He was always harried and panicked, racing between his three shops.	
He'd had an earlier start than me getting up at two a.m. to go to the wholesalers and pick up all the fresh produce.	Once he stripped a boy, tied him to a pillar and beat him with straps for stopping the machines.
Anne and Margaret always soothed him	We worked in link to tell each other when the overlooker was coming, with a code of signals so that we wouldn't get caught out.
the other shops would give us a phone call to let us know he was on his way so we could make sure everything looked perfect	

There are quite a few quotes, but this helps ensure you don't miss anything. From here, you can evaluate how useful, relevant or important each quote is.

Finally, you will **narrow down** again to find some **pairs of details**.

Paired details from Text A	Paired details from Text B
(The boss) was always harried and panicked, racing between his three shops… Anne and Margaret always soothed him The other shops would give us a phone call to let us know he was on his way so we could make sure everything looked perfect	Sometimes the overlooker is so angry with us he'll take one of the girls and beat her the full length of the room with a chain or with the strap. We worked in link to tell each other when the overlooker was coming, with a code of signals so that we wouldn't get caught out.

Once you have two pairs of matching quotes, it becomes much easier to respond to the question.

Summary

- Know exactly what you are looking for: highlight the key words in the question before you start.
- Read with a highlighter.
- Highlight specific words relating to the key focus.
- Look at the first sentence of each paragraph, decide whether it is likely to contain evidence relating to the key focus, then check the last sentence of each paragraph to verify.
- Look for key words or their synonyms.
- Move your eye quickly down the centre of the page.
- When you spot a key word, read the information around it carefully.
- Re-read the question to verify that the information you have found relates exactly to what you were asked.

~ Writers' choices about language ~

What you are being tested on

- Can you **identify interesting words and phrases** that contribute to effect?

- Can you **explain the ideas** in certain words or phrases?

- Can you **discuss the way the writer has used language** in fiction and non-fiction texts?

Sample task

Look again at **lines 11 to 20**. How does HG Wells use language to present the room?

You should use relevant subject terminology to support your answer.

Support your response with references to the text.

There were other and older stories that clung to the room, back to the half-credible beginning of it all, the tale of a timid wife and the tragic end that came to her husband's jest of frightening her. And looking around that large shadowy room, with its shadowy window bays, its recesses and alcoves, one could well understand the legends that had sprouted in its black corners, its germinating darkness. My candle was a little tongue of flame in its vastness that failed to pierce the opposite end of the room and left an ocean of mystery and suggestion beyond its island of light.

About the question

It will test your ability to **find information** in a **given part of the extract.** There will be lots of great examples of language there, so sometimes it can be hard to narrow down. Timing is often a problem as a result. Work out how many minutes you can spend on this question and know that you can write a paragraph of analysis every 4-6 minutes, so if you have an 8 mark question and 10 minutes to write, you could write 2 paragraphs of analysis. If you have a 12 mark question and 15 minutes to write, you could write 3 paragraphs of analysis. Stick carefully to your time allowance.

Understanding how you are marked

The mark scheme is divided into four:

1. Your use of **subject terminology.**
2. Your **use of quotation.**
3. Your **comments on the ideas and meanings of the text.**
4. Your **understanding of how language techniques work.**

How to improve your answer

The mark you are given is decided based on the quality of your comment on the language.

Do you have a clear understanding of **what the words used mean** or what they could **suggest**?

Do you know how the language features chosen by the writer help **share the meaning** of those words?

You also don't need to know complicated language features like alliteration or anaphora, metonymy or zeugma. Don't worry if you haven't a clue what a zeugma is!

Some of the best answers don't make reference to these things at all, and some of the weakest answers are littered with zeugmas and synecdoche. After all, being able to say *the writer uses plosive alliteration in the "tale of the timid wife"* sounds like it should get you a lot of marks, doesn't it? But what does the plosive alliteration do? That's the important bit.

What is being marked is your **quality of comment**.

So what is a comment?

A comment is what you say about the quotes that you pick out and the way the writer has used language.

In the following examples, we're going to explore the word 'sprouted' and how the legends 'sprouted' in the 'black corners' and 'darkness.'

Basic comments

The most simple and straightforward comments are **basic.** They are often generalised about the whole passage or true of a lot of writing.

The writer says the 'legends sprouted' which is a hook to make us want to read on.

The writer says the 'legends sprouted' which intrigues us.

The writer says the 'legends sprouted' which interests the reader.

The writer says the 'legends sprouted' which makes us curious and terrified.

These comments are very general. They could practically refer to most language ever written. In fact, if you find yourself saying the same kind of things in every single language question you answer, you probably fall into this trap. Avoid saying things like 'makes us want to read on' or that a word 'intrigues us' if you aren't explaining why.

Straightforward comments

Better comments are **straightforward**. That means you are trying to say something about the language, but it's probably not about the quote you have selected exactly, or you understand what the word means in general, but not in relation to this passage.

> The writer says the 'legends sprouted' which makes it sound like the darkness grew mysteriously.

> The writer says the 'legends sprouted' which grew and spread out.

> The writer says the 'legends sprouted' which is a metaphor making it seem like a plant that is growing.

'Sprouted' doesn't suggest growing mysteriously. Sprouting isn't mysterious. Sprouting could mean spreading out but that doesn't make sense when you think about legends. Legends don't spread out really, although they do grow as people share them. The final comment gets the idea, but doesn't really show any understanding of why the writer would have said that. It's very literal.

Straightforward comments often understand **what** the writer is doing but not **why**.

Successful comments

Successful comments show you know how to explain **what** the word means in relation to the passage, but also begin to explain **why** the writer chose that specific word or technique.

> The writer says the 'legends sprouted' which suggests the legends came into existence in the darkness, that they multiplied and **took root**. The darkness fed the legends like soil, air or fertiliser and nourished them so that they just kept growing.
>
>   The writer says the 'legends sprouted' in the shadows. This makes it sound as if the legends **came to life** in the shadows and that the darkness helped them **grow and flourish**.

Here, you can see that the students try to explain what 'sprouted' means by explaining **what** sprouted and **why** the writer would say that. They understand the big idea behind the words.

Skilful comments

For top marks, you will need to make **skilful** comments that are **developed and insightful**. **Developed** means you go on to develop your point. **Insightful** means you truly appreciate what the writer is doing.

> The writer says the 'legends sprouted' in the shadows. It sounds as if the shadows *took a seed of fear and that the shadowy darkness nourished that fear so that it 'germinated' and took root, feeding on the shadows and flourishing, coming to life.* The metaphor brings

those fears to life, showing how they could grow uncontrollably, **especially in such fertile circumstances.**

The writer says the 'legends sprouted' in the shadows. The stories that emerge from those dark, 'shadowy corners' seem to come into spontaneous existence and take root there, **like a weed that you are unable to dig out or kill off.**

Here, you can see that the student makes a developed comment in the first paragraph where they show they clearly understand WHY the writer has compared the ideas of legends to the idea of plants. They understand the point of comparison, the idea that connects legends to plants. They also understand that plants need fertile growing conditions to really grow very well and how that connects to the legends; They've also explained how the shadowy corners are perfect 'growing' conditions for those fears behind the stories.

In the second paragraph, the student is able to insightfully state that the fears grow 'like a weed' - that they are unwanted and unwelcome, but that they take over and get out of control, just like weeds do.

In other words, they really, really understand **why** the writer used that word we might see more in biology, 'sprouted' and 'germinated'.

If you're making **basic** comments, ban phrases like 'it makes you want to read on', 'it makes the reader curious', 'it engages us', 'it hooks us'.

So what do you write instead?

The best thing to do is **focus on one word** and explain what feeling or idea it shows. At a very basic level, you can do that by deciding if something is good or bad. Positive or negative.

When the writer says an 'island of light', **the word** 'light' **sounds** positive and warm.

Another way to improve if you've been making generalised comments about the passage is to **use a synonym** (and you can keep the feeling the word gives you as well).

When the writer says an 'island of light', **the word** 'light' **sounds** positive and warm. 'Light' **means** bright and cheery.

If you know what the technique is, you can put that in too, but only if you think it is important.

When the writer uses the metaphor 'island of light', **the word** 'light' **sounds** positive and warm. 'Light' **means** bright and cheery.

To move from **straightforward** to **successful** comments, you'll need to write about the word **in context**. That means in relation to the group of words you took it from.

When the writer uses the metaphor 'island of light', **the word** 'light' **sounds** positive and warm. 'Light' **means** bright and cheery, but as it is 'an island', that **makes us think that** the light is isolated and entirely surrounded by the darkness. The light sounds small and like it could easily be overwhelmed.

Can you see here how the student has tried to connect the idea of **light** to the idea of the island? With the word 'isolated', the student shows they understand the concept of islands - the reason why the writer has said it is an island. What is it about islands that connects with the man and his tiny candle in a dark shadowy room?

A further way to improve your marks is to **try to explain why the writer used a specific technique**. To do this, you need to understand why we use techniques. The phrase 'the [subject term] **helps us understand**' is often helpful here:

When the writer uses the metaphor 'island of light', the word 'light' sounds positive and warm. 'Light' means bright and cheery, but as it is 'an island', that makes us think that the light is isolated and entirely surrounded by the darkness. **The metaphor helps us understand** how solitary and cut off the writer feels by comparing the man and his candle to an 'island of light'.

This response shows a solid understanding of metaphors and what they do, as well as the idea of what is being compared.

If you're aiming for top marks, here, you're going to need to spend a little time getting to the central idea. Being insightful asks you to say something thoughtful that truly appreciates what the writer is trying to convey.

Let's look at **developed** first:

When the writer uses the metaphor 'island of light', **the word** 'light' **sounds** positive and warm. 'Light' **means** bright and cheery, but as it is 'an island', that **makes us think that** the light is **isolated** and entirely surrounded by the darkness. It suggests that the man is alone as 'island' sounds **tiny and insignificant** compared to the 'ocean of mystery and suggestion' **that surrounds them, as if it is inevitable**

that they will be surmounted by the darkness eventually. The metaphor helps us understand how solitary and cut off the writer feels **by comparing** the man and his candle to an 'island of light'.

You can see how the student has explored in detail the notion of island in comparison to the 'ocean of mystery and suggestion', as they have **added an additional comment** to the one they made in the previous sentence about being 'entirely surrounded'.

Making comments is not the only skill assessed in this question. There are also two other skills assessed that affect your comments: your **use of quotations** and **subject terminology**.

Weaker answers will tend to 'feature spot' subject terminology. That means they identify the feature and make a quote, but the comment is much less effective as they really have no idea why the technique has been used, or how the technique contributes to the idea.

To avoid this, look for good language first and <u>then</u> decide what it is, if you know. If you don't know or can't name it, don't worry. Some of the best answers aren't able to name what something is. If you know (and you are 100% sure) what your example is, then you can say what it is.

Even better is if you know **why** it's important. The problem is that words can be many, many things that you may have a job deciding which one of the terms is relevant and important.

Let's take the 'island of light' detail. So you might say 'island' is a noun. It is a noun, so you'd be right. You might also call it a metaphor but it IS kind of an island of light. But which is it? And even when we know what something is, it might not be relevant. Does being a noun contribute to the meaning? Or being a metaphor? Or both? And how? Tough questions to answer!

The best way to make a good comment about figurative language is to ask yourself:

"What does X have in common with Y?"

What does an island in an ocean have in common with a candle in the dark?

What do oceans have in common with mysteries?

What does a legend have in common with a seed that might sprout and germinate?

And the more you get to grips with that, the better your response is likely to be.

Because some students go into the exam looking for techniques, they often find things that are not relevant or can be difficult to explain. Alliteration or sibilance are two of those. Onomatopoeia is also hard to explain in context. Although you may feel you must write about the use of sentence forms such as fragments or complex sentences, this can also be very hard and lead to weaker, generalised responses.

The other aspect that you need to be conscious of is your use of quotation. It is often hard to navigate all of the wonderful use of language you will see in the selection. The person who writes the paper will pick out a bit that will be so very rich that you won't have the slightest problem finding words or phrases to write about. What is hard is narrowing down. Many students who struggle with this question would benefit from carefully reading the passage and spending a little time thinking about what details to select before narrowing down and focusing on two.

This is where you will use your close reading skills.

Your first selection might be very wide.

> There were other and older **stories that clung to the room**, back to the half-credible beginning of it all, the tale of a timid wife and the tragic end that came to her husband's jest of frightening her. And looking around that **large shadowy room, with its shadowy window bays**, **its recesses and alcoves, one could well understand the legends** **that had sprouted in its black corners, its germinating darkness.** **My candle was a little tongue of flame in its vastness** that failed to pierce the opposite end of the room and **left an ocean of mystery and** **suggestion beyond its island of light.**

Then **close read again and narrow down** by focusing on two main quotes with two smaller bits that may support you. Focus on smaller groups of words or phrases you might want to discuss, looking for a couple of main examples.

> There were other and older **stories that clung to the room,** back to the half-credible beginning of it all, the tale of a timid wife and the tragic end that came to her husband's jest of frightening her. And looking around that **large shadowy room, with its shadowy window bays**, **its recesses and alcoves, one could well understand the legends** **that had sprouted in its black corners, its germinating darkness.** **My candle was a little tongue of flame in its vastness** that failed to pierce the opposite end of the room and **left an ocean of mystery and** **suggestion beyond its island of light.**

The best answers show that the student has very carefully picked out some thoughtful quotations, then thought about what the writer is doing, their technique, before then writing about purpose and effect.

Example responses and commentary

Response 1

The writer uses a verb 'other and older stories clung to the room' to describe the room. This makes the room sound frightening and like it is grabbing at you. It makes you want to read on to find out what 'clung' to you and it hooks the reader.

   The writer also uses plosive sounds with 'in its black corners, its germinating darkness' which makes the room sound intriguing and scary.

The examples chosen are not very easy to write about. Although they have correctly identified the plosive sounds of 'black' and 'corners' they have only a simple understanding of why the writer may have done this. The comments on the quotes are simple and generalised as they could be about any part of the passage. The first comment on 'clung' is not really correct as we know already that it is the stories that clung to the room. Clung is correctly identified as a verb, but there is no real reason this is important to the meaning. The quotes are too long and the student has not focused in on one particular part of the quote.

Advice

To improve further, the student could:

- Write about a specific word and what it means or suggests.
- Avoid generalisations.
- Use shorter quotes.
- Focus on one word at a time.

Response 2

The writer uses a verb in 'other and older stories clung to the room' to describe the room. This verb 'clung' sounds unpleasant like the stories are gripping the room and won't let it go.

   The writer also uses a metaphor in 'oceans of mystery'. The word ocean sounds big and vast, and 'mystery' sounds like the room is full of secrets.

In this response, the student attempts to explain how 'clung' sounds, 'unpleasant' as well as offering a synonym, that they 'grip' the room. They correctly identify the metaphor, but oceans don't necessarily sound big or vast, though the student puts the word 'mystery' into their own words which shows some understanding.

Advice

To improve further, the student needs to:

- Write about **what** the writer's purpose is and **why** they might have used the technique.
- Write about the meaning in context with the whole sentence or idea.

Response 3

The writer uses a verb in 'other and older stories clung to the room' to personify the stories about the room. This verb 'clung' personifies the stories, making it sound as if they are grabbing onto the room and won't let go. It makes the legends around the room sound persistent and stubborn. The personification brings the stories to life, making them sound desperate and stubborn, as if they won't easily give in.

The writer also uses a metaphor in 'oceans of mystery'. The comparison focuses on how oceans are also often unfamiliar and unexplored, filled with mystery and danger, just like the darkness in the room. This helps us understand just how vast and unfamiliar the darkness is.

This answer uses relevant subject terminology that shows a solid understanding of what the writer is doing and why. They understand the technique used and the reason the writer has used it as well as the key ideas.

Advice

To improve further, the student could:

- Develop their ideas in more depth.

- Bring in other details that support their comments.

Response 4

The writer uses a verb in 'other and older stories clung to the room' personifying the stories that 'clung' to the room, grabbing persistently onto the room and won't let go. It makes the legends around the room sound persistent and stubborn. There is a sense with the verb that the stories are very much alive, unwilling to give up and refusing to give in. It makes it sound as if the stories are unlikely to give up their strong hold over the room and won't easily be dismissed.

The writer also uses a metaphor in 'oceans of mystery'. The comparison focuses on how oceans are also often unfamiliar and unexplored, filled with mystery and danger, just like the darkness in the room. This helps us understand just how vast and unfamiliar the darkness is. In comparison with the tiny 'island of light' from the candle, it makes it sound as if the narrator is very unlikely to conquer the darkness and the legends and stories attached to the room. We realise how easily this tiny 'island' could be wiped out or overcome by the darkness.

This answer is developed and insightful, with a solid understanding of the writer's technique and purpose.

Summary

- Avoid simple, generalised comments.
- Read through and make a broad selection of details.
- Then focus on two or three key quotes.
- Don't feature spot, but if you find one and it has been used for effect, then write about it.

Writers' choices in non-fiction texts

You will also be asked to explore how writers use language in non-fiction. This follows the exact same principles as the examples here for fiction.

Sample task

This question is about **Text B**

Look again at **lines 15 to 29**

Explore how the writer uses language to share her thoughts about the factory.

Support your response with detailed references to the text, using relevant subject terminology.

Basic comments

Like comments on fiction texts, some comments are limited and **basic.** They are often generalised about the whole passage or true of a lot of writing.

The writer uses a metaphor to say the engine room is the "beating heart of the mill" which compares the engine room to a beating heart **so we can picture what it is like.**

The writer uses a metaphor to say the engine room is the "beating heart of the mill" so **we know she feels afraid of it.**

The writer uses a metaphor to say the engine room is the "beating heart of the mill" so **we feel curious and terrified.**

Straightforward comments

Better comments are **straightforward**. That means you are trying to say something about the language, or using a synonym that shows some understanding but it's probably not about the right quote or you understand what the word means in general, but not in relation to this precise part of the passage.

> The writer uses a metaphor to say the engine room is the "beating heart of the mill" which **shows us the mill seemed alive**.

> The writer uses a metaphor to say the engine room is the "beating heart of the mill" which **makes it sound huge and powerful**.

With these comments, they are almost right but they are not in context and they haven't really understood the big ideas and concepts behind the words.

Straightforward comments often understand **what** the writer is doing but not **why**.

Successful comments

Successful comments show you know how to explain **what** the word means in relation to the passage, but also begin to think about **why** the writer chose that specific word.

> The writer uses a metaphor to say the engine room is the "beating heart of the mill" which shows us that the engine room is **the powerhouse of the mill,** to give the impression that **it is keeping everything else in motion.**

The writer uses a metaphor to say the engine room is the "beating heart of the mill" which shows us **how crucial** the engine house is, suggesting that the mill would be dead without it.

The writer uses a metaphor to say the engine room is the "beating heart of the mill" which **captures the steady, rhythmic yet powerful thumping** of the machine where the writer is suggesting the engine rooms metaphorically keep the mill alive.

Here, you can see that the students try to explain what the beating heart has in common with the engine rooms by explaining **what** the point of comparison is and **why** the writer would say that.

Skilful comments

If you're aiming for top marks, you will need to make **developed, insightful** comments.

The writer uses a metaphor to say the engine room is the "beating heart of the mill" which shows us how crucial the engine house is, suggesting that the mill would be dead without it. Because it's so vital to the life of the factory, the metaphor **suggests just how essential** the engine room is, and that **everything else depends on it**. When the writer adds "it never ceases", it makes it sound mechanical and eternal, but also unnatural, since a real human heart will keep beating but we'd expect the engine room to slow down sometimes. In all, it gives us the impression of **the mighty, unstoppable force** of the room **that seems to function in an unnatural and almost mysterious way**, because the writer does not tell us what powers the "heart", just that "it never ceases".

How to improve your answer

As with questions assessing your understanding of how writers use language in fiction, there are two other skills that are also assessed: your use of quotations and your use of subject terminology.

Look for good language first and **then** decide what it is, if you know. If you don't know or can't name it, don't worry. Some of the best answers aren't able to name what something is.

Even better is if you know **why** it's important.

Why is it interesting that the writer uses them?

For instance, if you spot some alliteration with "five o'clock the factory is in full movement", why are all these Fs interesting? You might even be more precise and call them fricatives. But that still doesn't answer the question about what's interesting about them. Some people might go on to say that there is an airy effect for fricatives, but that doesn't go with the meaning of this text which is very heavy and mechanical. Alliteration and onomatopoeia can be very hard to write thoughtfully about as it leads you to say very general things like 'it brings the text to life' or 'it allows us to imagine the sounds' and so on. However, if you do it well and these sound effects have contributed to the idea, that helps make a really strong answer.

Figurative language, verb choices and adverbs can be very useful to explore as they convey more of the idea of the writing.

The other aspect that you need to think about is your use of quotation.

Start by **underlining or highlighting the key words** of the question.

How does the writer use language to **describe the factory**?

Then start your close reading, **underlining or highlighting everything that relates to the key focus**.

Our hours were six in the morning to seven at night, but I worked from five in the morning until nine at night when we were busy, and that was most days. **The engine room is the beating heart of the mill,** and everything after is **a noisy wave of click-clacking machines, pistons, pumps, gears, levers, cogs, spindles, cranks, flywheels, throttles and valves. It never ceases. By five o'clock the factory is in full movement.** A wind-fan gives us **an infernal fog of heat and moisture**. Everything moves in a **constant whirring motion** and **a stench of fumes hangs in the air**. It is often intolerable. There is no time for breakfast or drinking. We do as we can when the machines are running and we are often famished. **The factory is a sort of prison-house** as once the mill gates are locked, you cannot come or go. We are given forty minutes for our meal at noon. The food is very ordinary and not plentiful. Many of us are half-starved.

Once you have done this, **go back and narrow down three or four key ideas** that you want to explore. Make sure you consider the details equally across the whole passage that you've been given.

Our hours were six in the morning to seven at night, but I worked from five in the morning until nine at night when we were busy, and that was most days. **The engine room is the beating heart of the mill,** and everything after is **a noisy wave of click-clacking machines, pistons, pumps, gears, levers, cogs, spindles, cranks, flywheels, throttles and valves. It never ceases. By five**

o'clock the factory is in full movement. A wind-fan gives us **an infernal fog of heat and moisture**. Everything moves in a **constant whirring motion** and **a stench of fumes hangs in the air**. It is often intolerable. There is no time for breakfast or drinking. We do as we can when the machines are running and we are often famished. **The factory is a sort of prison-house** as once the mill gates are locked, you cannot come or go. We are given forty minutes for our meal at noon. The food is very ordinary and not plentiful. Many of us are half-starved.

You can also look for words that fit together, such as the ones to do with sound or smell.

The best answers show that the student has very carefully picked out some thoughtful quotations on the given focus, then thought about what the writer is doing, their technique, before then writing about purpose and effect.

Example responses and commentary

Response 1

Firstly, in the first lines of this extract, the writer uses contrast to talk about her experiences of factory work. A quote for this is 'Our hours were six in the morning to seven at night, but I worked from five in the morning until nine at night', this shows the writer has used shocking contrast to show the hard hours of these workers: she was supposed to work for 13 hours in the factory, but instead she ended up doing 16 hours regularly. This suggests if she was still doing 16 hours, she would be tired and would not get enough sleep and she would have to wake up at 4 in the morning.

   Next the writer uses alliteration to describe her experiences of factory work and what the machines are doing. A quote for this is 'everything after is a noisy wave of click-clacking machines'. The word 'click clacking' is an onomatopoeia. This effect on the reader means we can hear the machines in our heads and the quote 'click clacking' tells us that the factory machines will carry on.

This response hasn't really focused on very interesting details. Instead, the student has started by thinking about what language features they can identify, then found examples of those. Alliteration is not the easiest technique to focus on, and whilst the student may be right that there is some alliteration, we are left to guess which of the words use alliteration. They are right that 'click-clacking' uses onomatopoeia but they have little understanding of why the writer would do that.

Advice

To improve further, this student needs to:

- Pick out interesting language rather than trying to find examples of language features.

- Avoid generalised comments.

- Focus in on individual words and make a better selection of detail.

Response 2

Firstly, the writer uses a long list of nouns to describe her experiences of factory work. A quote for this is 'pistons, pumps, gears, levers, cogs', this suggests that these are all part of a machine in the factory and the writer uses a lot of machinery nouns of what's happening. The effect of this is there will be a constant noise of movements, as all the parts are working together. The long list helps us imagine how many parts there are.

Secondly, the writer uses a metaphor to describe her experiences of factory work. A quote for this is 'The factory is a sort of prison-house'. The effect on this reader tells us that she is describing how trapped people working there are.

This response, while brief, correctly identifies one language feature, the long list of nouns. The second is perhaps a metaphor, but as discussed previously, it is not clear if the writer means this metaphorically or not. The details chosen are more interesting than the previous response, and there is some understanding of the ideas and perspectives conveyed by them shown by the comments. In the first paragraph, there is a straightforward explanation of why the writer has used a long list.

Advice

To improve further, this student needs to:

- Focus on **why** the writer has specific language.

- Be selective with the choice of quotation.

- Focus in on which particular words give specific effects.

Response 3

In the passage the writer uses language to describe working in the mill as very brutal and is clearly a physical struggle. The writer states that "A wind-fan gives us an infernal fog of heat" while they are working. Here, the work is made to seem like hell and like the worst torture with the word, "infernal" which refers to the underworld where people are sent to be punished. The metaphor works to suggest that the work is so rough and horrible that you should try to avoid it at all costs just like hell.

The writer goes on to portray the workplace as negative. The worker is clearly affected by, "a stench of fumes [that] hangs in the air" for its prominence in the difficulty of the work. The use of the word, "stench" has connotations to suggest that the smell is almost overpowering in a bad way as it is so bad. This adds to the reasons as to why working there is so brutal, because of the fact that it is hard to breathe within these, "fumes" that "hang" in the air. The fact that the fumes are described as, "hang[ing]" is significant as it suggests that the air is almost dead as though it has just been hung.

Finally, not only is the workplace described as a place of punishment in a metaphorical sense with the word, "infernal", it described as though physically there is no way out. The writer states that, "The factory is a sort of prison-house...you cannot come or go", which adds to the idea that physically you are trapped there once the "gates are locked." The fact that it is described as a, "prison" suggests that this should be a place for the worst kind of people that deserve to be punished rather than those that simply need some money. She goes on to suggest that even though the factory workers are in constant suffering and feel as though they're being unfairly punished, they have no other choice; they are bound by this system and cannot escape until the debt is paid.

This student clearly identifies particular words and focuses on the key words in the examples they explore. They are correct in their identification of language features, as well as the main ideas. They accurately explore the idea behind the word 'infernal' although their attempt to explain why a metaphor has been used is less effective. They give away some of the idea in the statement which helps establish a solid understanding of the ideas, but there is no successful understanding of the writer's use of language.

Advice

To improve further, this student needs to:

- Explore in more detail why language features have been chosen.
- Explore the quotation in context.
- Link the choice of the language feature to the idea being conveyed.
- Think about timing: this is a very long response.

Response 4

Elizabeth's Ogden's experiences of factory work are shown to be very labour intensive and physically straining. Even the sentences convey a certain weariness and a sense of the ceaselessness that she has to go through every day with the use of listing, such as with the four clause sentence spanning one and half lines from line 16 to 17 which mimics the large span of time from 'six in the morning to seven at night' that her factory work takes, emphasizing the length and ceaseless nature of the day. Moreover, this is even more apparent in lines 15-17, where the long listing of the machinery and objects that she has to work with gives a sense of how overwhelming all of the 'noisy' parts of the engine room are and it is as though harsh sibilance and the plosives of the 's'-ending 'pistons' and 'pumps' emulates the hard, deafening mechanical sounds of the factory so that we can understand just how many layers there are to all this 'infernal' mechanical noise. This consequently makes the factory seem very brutal and intense for the character.

The use of description also gives a sense of the horrendous conditions that Elizabeth and the workers have to face with such adjectives of 'infernal', 'intolerable' being used, as well as the description of the factory being a 'prison-house'. The emphasis of 'Infernal', from the writer, suggests that the factory relates to the horrors of hell and the underworld and intolerable as the work being impossible to be endured, not just a type of punishment but a form of torture. These connotations of evil and horror, stress the dreadful experience, making us feel deep pity for the narrator and feel that the factory work is inhumanly cruel. This is reinforced then with the idea of it being a 'prison-house' and therefore that they are trapped and kept as though they are criminals and have done something wrong, but the adjective 'infernal' gives us a sense that this is something beyond human punishments in a prison, but something designed to break their spirits for eternity.

In the first paragraph, the student shows perceptive understanding of the use of longer sentences with multiple clauses, as well as perceptive understanding of the use of sound. If you compare this with the basic responses in the first answer, you can see how to discuss the use of sound in meaningful ways.

Summary

- Put a box around the text for the lines identified in the question.
- Identify the focus of the question.
- Use close reading to identify all potentially useful or relevant quotations.
- Narrow down on the most useful examples of language.
- Avoid simple, generalised comments and feature spotting.
- Focus on the effect of language: what it means, what the big idea is, what it suggests and what impression it gives.
- Avoid generalised comments about how it makes the reader feel. In general we don't feel shocked, surprised, angry or fearful when we read.

~ Writers' choices about structure ~

When composing, writers make choices about the sequence and position of their ideas that support meaning. At GCSE you are expected to understand the way in which writers structure texts at both paragraph and whole-text level.

In order to explore writers' structural choices in more detail, you will need to read Text C on page 176 before you start.

In some questions, you will be expected to write about structure when you write about language, just as you do in GCSE English Literature. In others, you may be asked about structure in a question on its own. Make sure you understand which approach your exam board requires before you start.

You may, of course, choose to write about structure in the longer questions comparing two texts or in the essay-style question asking you to make a personal critical response to a piece of writing.

You will need to show understanding of key aspects of narrative structure, such as chronology. You will also need to show understanding of how writers organise non-chronological non-fiction writing.

What you are being tested on

- Can you identify how the writer has **sequenced or developed** their ideas?
- Can you can explain why the writer has **positioned** something where they did?
- Can you **pick out parts** of the text and use them in your answer to discuss the way the writer has used structure?

Essentially, can you explain <u>why</u> the writer has done something at a specific point in the text?

About the question

It will test your ability to work across the **whole of the extract** or, in some cases **a shorter given section.** If you are writing about structural techniques the writers have used in a comparison of two whole texts, you may be working with a huge amount of text.

For that reason, this guide will start by looking at structure within a smaller section of the text before working up to compare structure across two whole texts. Whilst this may not always be relevant for your exam course, the skills are the same and you should find that what you learn about analysing one block of text will apply to other lengths of section too.

If you are writing about fiction in your exam, remember that the paper will almost always give you an extract. That is helpful in many ways. The passage selected will have been carefully chosen so that there are interesting aspects of structure for you to explore. The ending will often be a carefully chosen stopping point in the text that should allow you to answer this question well.

Timing can be a real problem with questions that assess structure because they can ask you to handle the whole text. That in itself is very demanding in a short amount of time.

The question can also be made more difficult if you're trying to use lots of over-complicated subject terminology. If you're writing about sentences, that can also take up a lot of your time and not gain you any marks. To be clear, structure in this guide refers to the organisation of everything **larger than** the sentence. If you're writing about structure within a sentence, you're really working at word level with language.

Understanding how you are marked

Assessment is divided up into three areas.

1. Your **use of subject terminology.**
2. Your **use of details.**
3. Your **comments on the structure** of the text.

There is no need to use complex terminology but there are blocks of words that will really help you write well.

How to improve your answer

There are **three types of words** that are particularly helpful when discussing structure in fiction or narrative texts: **chronological words** that help us explore how things progress, **comparative words** that help us articulate how things change or develop, and **adverbs** that help us explain how ideas are introduced or change.

Chronological words
Adverbials for openings: at first, at the beginning, first of all, initially, to begin with, first, at the outset, to start with, before all else, in the first place.
Verbs for openings: creates, establishes, starts.
Adverbials for progression: next, later, after, consequently, following this, after, as soon as, at last, subsequently, after a while, as things unfold.
Verbs for progression: unfolds, develops, evolves, intensifies, extends, elaborates, deepens, changes, shifts, unravels, discovers, complicates, clarifies.

Adverbials for reference to other time points: previously, before, up to now, until now, prior to this, earlier, henceforth, from this point on, from now on, already, subsequently, later.

Adverbials for endings: finally, eventually, at the end, ultimately, at last, in the end, at the close, by and by, lastly, at length, at the last moment.

Verbs for endings: concludes, finishes with, builds up to, reveals, closes, ends, resolves, determines, settles.

Comparative words
Even more, even less, -er adjectives, comparative adjectives, less, more.

Adverbs and adverbial phrases about how an idea is introduced
All of a sudden, eventually, suddenly, gradually, predictably, unexpectedly.

Another type of word, **hierarchical words** also help us explain how writers prioritise or rank order ideas in non-narrative writing. Good answers will make use of all these and you'll be able to spot these in the student responses later.

These words also help you explain the crucial aspect of structure. What you need to explain is: why this, here, now?

What **changes**? What **develops**? What is **introduced and how**? What does this detail help us understand before or after?

Let's have a look at a paragraph from the Text C on page 176.

> I decided to make a systematic examination of the place. I began to walk about the room, peering round each article of furniture, tucking up the sheets of the bed, and opening its curtains wide. I pulled up the blinds and examined the fastenings of the several windows before closing the shutters, leant forward and looked up the blackness of the wide chimney, and tapped the dark oak panelling for any secret opening.

We'll take each sentence in turn:

The sentence	What is this?	Why tell us this here?
I decided to make a systematic examination of the place.	An explanation of the narrator's actions	So that we understand why he's walking about and what he's doing. It explains the narrator's thoughts.
I began to walk about the room, peering round each article of furniture, tucking up the sheets of the bed, and opening its curtains wide.	A description of what the narrator does	So that we understand just how systematic an examination he made; that he was really looking for a human not a ghost.
I pulled up the blinds and examined the fastenings of the several windows before closing the shutters, leant forward and looked up the blackness of the wide chimney, and tapped the dark oak panelling for any secret opening.	A further description of what the writer does	So that we understand just how thorough he was and how he left no stone unturned. It exemplifies his 'systematic examination'.

When it comes to writing about structure, you take these ideas and some of the helpful structural words to explain why the writer does this, here, now. It can also be helpful to think about what we'd miss out on if the writer *didn't* tell us this, here, now.

For example:

> The writer **starts the paragraph** by telling us that the narrator made a "systematic examination" of the room, **which helps us understand** his actions in the **subsequent sentences. Without this** insight into his actions, **we wouldn't understand** as clearly what he is doing or why. We can also see, through the use of the word "systematic" in this first sentence, just how rigorous his search is. **Next**, the narrator outlines the places he searched and how, checking behind the blinds and curtains, under the bed, and even checking the wall for false panels. From this, we understand just how systematic his search was. He becomes even more thorough **as the paragraph develops. This clarifies** how carefully and diligently he carries out the examination **mentioned in the first sentence.**

Using **comparative language, phrases that mark chronology and position**, as well as explaining what the position of this idea **helps us understand earlier or later** in the paragraph, you will be able to explain clearly and in-depth why the writer has sequenced the ideas in the way that they have.

When working with a longer section of text, or the whole text itself, the main challenge is to narrow down three areas where the position of the ideas is particularly relevant. It's not possible to do the detailed analysis you've seen in the previous example when you are discussing the whole text.

The easiest way to do this is to focus on a single aspect of the opening, a turning point and then the ending. From the Text C on page 107, there are many aspects you could choose to explore in more detail.

The most important thing is covering the whole of the section or text you are given. It's not sufficient in this question to explore structure just at the beginning or in the middle. For that, you will need to select carefully.

What stands out in the text as being important?

Why this, here, now?

This could be a detail, or a bit of information.

- Why tell us 'the young duke had died' at the beginning?
- Why tell us he makes a systematic search of the room before the action starts?
- Why tell us that he lit all the candles in the middle?
- Why keep repeating about the shadows?

This could also be a structural technique as well.

- Changes from a big focus to a small focus, narrowing in, zooming out: why focus on a specific tiny detail?
- Shifts of time, topic, person or place.
- Sudden introductions or changes.
- Gradual introductions or changes.
- Turning points.
- Flashforwards & flashbacks.
- Foreshadowing.
- External actions of characters and internal thoughts of characters.
- Shifting point of view.

- Circular structures.
- Build-ups.
- Cliffhangers.
- Change or intensification of mood.
- Shifts between action or dialogue or description.
- Rising action, exposition, climax.

Why have this idea or this structural feature here, and why now?

It can be helpful to **identify** the structural technique, say **where** it comes in the passage in terms of beginning, middle or end, and then try to **explain** why you think the writer has done this.

Basic comments

Basic comments are the most simple responses. Students who do this will write things like:

At the beginning, the writer says that he had "a sudden twinge of apprehension" *which intrigues us and makes us want to read on.*

Straightforward comments

Straightforward comments are better. Students who do this will write things like:

At the beginning, the writer says that he had "a sudden twinge of apprehension" *so that we understand the narrator is afraid. At first, he feels nervous but then this changes and he is in a state of "considerable nervous tension". There is a turning point when the* writer says "After midnight" *which is spooky and the candles start to blow out.*

Here, the student may identify **what** the structural feature is. They can also identify some of the changes that happen in the story and have **some understanding about what the effect is**.

Successful comments

Successful comments are even better. Students who do this will write things like:

At the beginning, the writer says that he had "a sudden twinge of apprehension" *so that we understand the narrator is already nervous even though nothing has happened.* At first, he feels nervous but then this changes and he is in a state of "considerable nervous tension" *which helps us understand that he is becoming more and more tense despite the fact there is "no cause for this condition".* There is a turning point when the writer says "After midnight" and the dialogue "By Jove!" shows us that although the narrator is trying to stay cheerful and positive, "in a leisurely manner", the pace that the candles go out quickens and he becomes frantic as he tries to keep the candles alight.

Here, the student clearly understands **what techniques the writer is using** and **why** the writer has put them where they are. They **explain successfully what the effect is**.

Skilful comments

Developed and **insightful** comments are the gold standard. To do this, you also need to have a clear overview of the whole text. That means you can offer a summary of the changes. Another way students often excel is by writing generally and then becoming specific with particular details. You may also have the ability to discuss the mood and atmosphere, or track changes and developments.

> In the passage, we see the narrator battle between feeling nervous or 'apprehensive' *at the beginning* and trying to be factual and practical. He shifts from one to the other, *but eventually* the mystery of the room begins to affect him.

This is an **overview**. It's a good way to start your response to reach higher marks. This is already a clear understanding of the shifts of the passage. You can do this whether you are asked to focus on a couple of paragraphs or on the whole passage.

To cover the whole passage, you really need to have details from the beginning, a turning point and the end. That also helps you have an overview of the whole text and reach higher levels.

> *At the beginning,* the narrator **describes** his feelings to us, **giving us his internal emotions**, saying 'I had a sudden twinge of apprehension', which tells us that he felt a little nervous. **His descriptions of the shadows and the darkness help us understand why he feels this way** even though he makes a 'systematic evaluation of the place' even checking under the bed and behind the curtains to make sure there is

nobody there who is playing tricks on him, just like the 'husband' and his 'jest' of frightening his wife.

In this paragraph, the student describes **what** the writer is doing (underlined) and gives an example which is then explained (bold). The student already understands what the writer is doing and **why**.

When the writer reveals that the narrator had made a 'kind of barricade' and got out his revolver, it sounds as if he is prepared for everything and as if he thinks the cause of these legends is probably human. The writer gives us all the details of the narrator's external actions so that we know he's investigated every angle, that he's checked for hidden panels and places a person could hide. He 'looked up' the chimney and 'tapped' the panels so that we know he's done the search properly. He also gets more candles and makes sure there are no shadows anywhere to put his mind at rest. This helps us understand exactly why he reacts as he does at the turning point, when 'one of the candles in the alcove suddenly went out'.

At first, he is calm and rational, as we see from his speech, as he thinks it is a 'draught', but then when the 'two candles' were 'extinguished' on the little table, he begins to panic. Because we know he has already checked the room out thoroughly, we know there isn't a person doing this, and the way the narrator describes it as 'extinguished' and 'suddenly' as well as the way they have not been 'blown out' but snuffed out, 'as if between a finger and thumb' gives the impression at the end that there is something human-like at work in the room, something supernatural.

We finish on a cliffhanger, not knowing if the narrator ever gets to the bottom of the mystery, whether it was just a breeze that had blown them out or whether someone was playing a trick on him. But because we know he had 'examined' the room carefully and that the candles seem to have been snuffed out rather than blown out by the wind, we are left with no alternative, like the narrator, but to think it is because something supernatural is at work and that there was something in all the shadows after all.

By the end of the answer, it is clear that this student has a sense of the passage as a whole and that they know **what** the writer has done and **why**, what the effects are. They are detailed and they use quotation **judiciously** to compose an argument relating to the mystery at the end.

These skills are the same with non-fiction and non-narrative texts.

You may also be asked to explore structure across the whole text. Structure is also considered a technique writers use to create meaning, so even if you do not have an explicit question asking about structure in non-fiction texts, you may still wish to write about it in a comparative question or a longer essay question.

Let's look at non-fiction texts, starting with Text A on page 170. Take a quick read-through just to remind yourself of the passage before we start.

In both fiction and non-fiction, you can explore structure across a whole text very simply. To do that, compare the opening and the ending, exploring how the writer arrives at their final message. In Text A, you could explore why the writer takes the structural approach that she does to arrive at her main point.

By the time I was twelve, I got my first job, working a milk round before school. We were up at 5 a.m. to make sure all the milk had gone out, clinging onto the back of a milk float* and racing to catch up if we'd left a couple of pints at the bottom of a long driveway. It's no wonder I found school so exhausting. Next came a Saturday job in a greengrocer's shop when I was thirteen, helping stack up the fruit and vegetables. Between the two jobs, that gave me enough every week to buy a couple of magazines, a couple of music singles or a poster of my favourite bands. When I was sixteen, I started working in a local restaurant and then in a bar at eighteen. Those jobs were much less strenuous, that's for sure.

Those first jobs gave me a real appreciation of work and the value of money. I might get celebrity treatment these days as a TV presenter, but I'll always be proud of how hard I worked to get where I am.

You can also look for the same discourse markers that you will be using to write about structure: chronology, progression, development, comparison and adverbs to express how things changed.

Here, looking at the writer's final statement about being proud of how hard she worked to get where she is, a student then looks back at the opening paragraph to explore how the writer builds up to the final idea.

The writer finishes by telling us that she is proud of how hard she worked, knowing that it has helped her as an adult. She concludes by saying that she now has "a real appreciation of work and the value of money." Because she opens the passage by explaining the difficulties of working when she was young, that she started when she was 12, that she had to start work at 5am on a school day and that it gave her "enough" to buy "a couple of magazines, a couple of music singles or a poster", we understand why she later says she understands "the value of money" as an adult, as she clearly did a physically exhausting job to earn a bit of pocket money. The opening helps us understand how she came to appreciate how hard you have to work sometimes in return for very little.

Here, the student has picked out a detail from the end of the passage and looked at how the opening helps the reader understand the writer's perspective. What is also important to understand is that the student may be commenting on words and ideas but they are exploring the position and order of those ideas, not what the words or language features contribute to the meaning. You can never divorce structure from language entirely.

Example responses and commentary

Let's return to the extract from Text C.

Response 1

The writer focuses our attention at the beginning of the story on the castle and how it is full of dark and shadows so that the reader has a clear understanding of where the character is and what he is like. They then change the focus as the text develops and focus on the candles so that the reader has some idea about what could happen and how the writer is trying to intrigue the reader to make it sound mysterious. The writer uses different types of structural features to engage the reader and make us want to read on.

The comments in this answer are **basic** and **generalised**. The student identifies some simple details about the dark, shadows and the candles. They also make a better comment about it sounding mysterious, but it is very generalised and not related to the text. The answer uses the bullet points in the question to start each sentence, but what they write could relate to most texts.

Advice

To improve further, this student needs to:

- Pick out specific details.
- Try to comment on specific effects.
- Avoid making simple, generalised comments.

Response 2

The writer begins the text by focusing on the narrator who is standing outside the red room and who is clearly feeling nervous. This interests the reader as it shows us that the narrator is feeling scared before they even go into the room. This engages us because we want to know why he is feeling so worried.

Then the writer changes the focus and describes the shadows in the room and the legends about the room. It changes to a more mysterious description to make us feel worried for the narrator and wonder if he will still be alive at the end.

Towards the end, the candles begin to go out one by one and the narrator is in a clear panic. This makes us worried for the narrator and wonder what will happen to him.

Here, the student is using specific details from the passage. They pick out a detail and then they show some understanding of what the effect is on the reader at each point in the story. There are several straightforward comments that show some understanding of the position of ideas.

Advice

To improve the response, the student needs to:

- Use subject terminology.
- Show they understand **what** the writer is doing and **why**.
- Treat all parts of the text not just the opening and the ending.

Response 3

At the beginning of the text, the narrator describes the setting as well as his internal feelings, saying he was 'in a shadowy corner' which helps us understand why he had a 'sudden twinge of apprehension'. Then the narrator reveals the legends about the young duke, about the frightened wife and 'other and older stories that clung to the room' which helps us understand why the narrator feels anxious and a little afraid.

The writer then switches to giving us the details of the narrator's external actions, checking the chimney, shutting the shutters and checking for hidden passages so that we understand he conducted a thorough search. The writer tells us this here so that later, we trust that there isn't someone going around putting the candles out as a joke or trick. It also helps us understand that the narrator tries to 'reassure' himself but he still feels on edge.

Later in the story, as the candles begin to blow out one by one, the writer introduces dialogue so that we can see how the narrator is trying to keep cheerful and not give into his fears, but that he starts to panic as the candles go out. The way he describes the candles at the end helps us understand that they weren't blown out by accident but that they seem to have been put out on purpose, which adds to the mystery and helps us understand the narrator's fear.

This student has a real grasp of what happens and where, as well as the main actions. They know what the writer is doing and comprehend what it helps us understand at each point. They are clearly aware of the position of ideas and how structural features contribute to meaning.

Advice

To improve further, this student needs to:

- Write an overview or summary.

- Discuss mood.

- Track the changing mood and explain how the writer creates those changes.

Response 4

The passage takes us from the first moments of a scary night with a practical yet 'apprehensive' narrator to leave us on a tense cliffhanger with the narrator at a realisation that there may be something supernatural at work.

At the beginning, the mood is edgy and uncertain. The writer presents the external actions of the narrator, as well as his internal thoughts through the first-person narrative viewpoint, so that we know he was not only investigating the 'shadowy corners' in a methodical way, but also we get an insight into his feelings, that he felt a 'sudden twinge of apprehension', so that we understand he is practical and sensible but that he is not immune to the powers of the room. By telling us that his candle was a 'little tongue of flame' in the 'vastness' of the room, we realise that it is unlikely he is going to be able to conquer his fears, despite his determination to do so. The way he methodically examines the room 'peering around the furniture' and checking under the beds should reassure both the narrator and us that there is nobody in the room who could be playing a practical joke on us, but by ruling out any possibility of human pranks with a 'locked' door, no secret panels, shuttered windows and this 'systematic' search, what the writer has done is rule out any reason for the candles to seem like they have been put out by human hands later. That makes it especially eerie when we finish with a cliffhanger that the wicks seemed to have been snuffed out neatly 'as if between a finger and a thumb'. It's only because we know he was so thorough in the search that we are forced to consider the possibility of a supernatural explanation.

The writer also uses the structure to create a metaphorical war between light and shadow, with the 'tongue' of the candle in the 'vastness' of the shadows at the beginning, the lighting of the fire and all the candles, then the addition of other candles so that 'not one inch of the room darkened', it seems at this point as though the narrator has won the battle against the darkness that he has earlier told us is ripe for 'germinating' legends. However when the candle blows out 'suddenly' and leaves a 'black shadow' that 'sprang' back, we realise that this is just the first step in a battle against the darkness that he is unlikely to win. It's not just a battle between light and dark, however, as it is also the same battle between reason and sense versus emotion and fear. The speed at which the shadows come back makes it unlikely he'll win and he'll be unable to keep relighting them quickly enough. It also means his fears and 'apprehension' will inevitably win out. The cliffhanger also leaves us certain that the narrator will lose his battle against the darkness and his fears, as well as being sure there is something more than human at work.

This answer is comprehensive, covering many of the subtleties of the structure. It is detailed and developed, being able to track the changes and progression of the text. There is an insightful understanding about what the writer is doing and why, eliminating all doubt of human intervention, as well as the way in which the battle between light and shadow, reason and emotion is structured. The student needs to be careful they don't risk over-answering the question: spending too much time on this question could cost them marks later in the paper.

Summary

- Avoid simple, generalised comments.

- Track through moods and changes.

- Identify structural features then think about why the writer has used them.

- Make sure you cover the whole of the text as best you can in the time.

- Try to think in terms of 'Because the writer has told us **this**, **here**, it helps us understand … later on'.

- Use lots of structural words to help you explain **when** the writer does something.

- Try to make sure you open or conclude with a sentence that summarises the changes or developments from beginning to end.

~ Making critical comparisons ~

In your exam, you will be asked to write a critical comparison of two texts. Usually, this type of task will ask you to write for between 15-25 minutes. They ask you to compare or contrast the viewpoints of the writers as well as the techniques they use to share their ideas.

What you are being tested on

- Can you **identify the writer's viewpoint** and **explore how they created it**?
- Can you pick out relevant details **across two passages**?
- Can you write **a close comparison** focusing on a given theme or idea?
- Can you **identify and explain** how the writer has used techniques for effect?

Sample task

For this question, you need to refer to the **whole of Text A**, together with the **whole of Text B.**

Both of these texts are about working as a teenager.

What are the differences between these experiences of the world of work?

Explore:

- Their different perspectives on work
- The techniques they use to get their experiences across to the reader

Use evidence from **both** texts to support your answer.

About the question

The question will ask you to focus on both texts and has a much broader focus than the short questions asking you to find evidence and infer meaning from two texts. Remember that you have to do two things with this question: compare AND write about the writers' techniques. If you miss one aspect of this out, you will not be able to access all the marks available. This is a **critical** comparison of two texts.

Understanding how you are marked

There are three components that are assessed as part of your response.

1. Find **comparable aspects** of the **writers' ideas and perspectives.**

2. Find **evidence** to help support your response.

3. Discuss the **methods/techniques**.

Like other questions, your final mark depends on whether your comparison of the perspectives and your understanding of techniques is **basic**, **straightforward**, **successful** or **skilful**.

How that looks in students' responses:

	Comparison	and	Understanding of Technique
Basic response	Simple identification of the similarities or differences in ideas and perspectives		Simple identification of **what** the writer is doing
Straightforward response	Some understanding of the similarities or differences in ideas and perspectives		Accurate identification of **what** the writer is doing
Successful response	Sound understanding of the similarities in ideas and perspectives		Accurate understanding of **what** the writer is doing and **why**
Skilful response	Developed and insightful understanding of the similarities in ideas and perspectives		Developed and insightful understanding of **what** the writer is doing and **why**

How to improve your answer

First, **identify the key words** of the question.

> What are the **differences** between these experiences of **the world of work**?

Then scan through and **find your evidence**. Read through and identify all the evidence that shows the writer's thoughts, opinions or feelings.

You may find it helpful to **use two different colours** or methods - one for positive perspectives, and one for negative perspectives. This can help you gain an overall image or track any changes.

Here a student has made their selection and picked out positive quotes (highlighted) and negative quotes (underlined). When scanning, remember your aim is to make a wide selection.

Text A	Text B
The milk round wasn't bad work, even though it was an early start. In the summer, though, there were definite benefits to being up early It left me with a deep love of those early summer mornings and even now I'm an early bird rather than a night owl	It is often intolerable. We do as we can when the machines are running We were always frightened of getting the strap or not getting paid,

~ Reading skills; Making critical comparisons ~

I can't say the winters were as joyous. We might never have seen our customers, but we definitely felt appreciated. They taught me ... and how work didn't have to be serious Those first jobs gave me a real appreciation of work and the value of money. I'll always be proud of how hard I worked to get where I am.	Mill work is very hard I cannot tell you the pain and weariness but I know most of the doffers have pains like that. The hardship and cruelty I've known in that mill since I was a girl is too much to carry.

Once you have scanned the texts, you will then need to **read closely**, appraising the details that you have found and making links. You should end with between 4 and 8 comparable quotes from both texts for the whole essay.

Remember, the more you have truly weighed up the evidence, the more likely you are to be successful. Good answers start with good evidence.

Then link up the quotes together:

Text A	Text B
The milk round wasn't bad work, even though it was an early start.	I cannot tell you the pain and weariness but I know most of the doffers have pains like that.
Those first jobs gave me a real appreciation of work and the value of money.	The hardship and cruelty I've known in that mill since I was a girl is too much to carry.
We might never have seen our customers, but we definitely felt appreciated.	We were always frightened of getting the strap or not getting paid,
It left me with a deep love of those early summer mornings and even now I'm an early bird rather than a night owl	We do as we can when the machines are running

You will be doing this directly on the text so it should be very quick.

Once you have your shortlist, you can then **start writing your response**.

Make sure you are clear about your exam syllabus and how much they expect you to write in the time. For a question worth 10% of the final marks on the paper, you will not be expected to write in as much depth as a paper that requires you to spend 20% of your time on writing a critical comparison. That will affect the number of quotations that you have time to explore in your comparison.

Of the quotations you choose, always **prioritise the most important ones** and make an order out of your quotes. This helps you with time management: it is unlikely you will be able to cover everything you would like to write and so if you start from the beginning with your main point, you won't suffer if you run out of time because you were tackling the less important points of comparison.

It's very helpful to **start with a general comment about both texts** as an opening to each paragraph. You can state similarities or differences in their approach if you like and give a little away in regards to what you would say about the texts. You should also use the words of the question.

> **Both writers focus on some of the problems of working as a teenager,** although in Text A, those problems are relatively minor and in Text B, they are very serious.

There is a focus on the question (underlined) and a simple point of comparison (in bold).

From this, you can **explore either Text A or Text B in more detail**. You may want to take up the idea from the opening sentence for the text you start to work with. There is no reason you have to do text A or B first. In fact, it may help you to work with the one that has the clearest viewpoint or a technique that is easiest to explore.

For this point, the student has paired two quotes:

The milk round wasn't bad work, even though it was an early start.	I cannot tell you the pain and weariness but I know most of the doffers have pains like that.

Since the quote from Text A is not particularly interesting, dramatic or full of meaning, it makes more sense for this point to start with Text B.

Both writers focus on some of the problems of working as a teenager, although in Text A, those problems are relatively minor and in Text B, they are very serious. In Text B, she cannot even find the words to describe "the pain and weariness" she feels. The way she describes the "weariness" of the work makes it sound as if it is not just tiring, but it completely exhausts her to such a point that she doesn't even know how to describe it. It is such hard work that it's not only left her drained and weak, but unable to work anymore.

Here, the student is focusing in on Text B and drilling down into the text by focusing on the "weariness". At the point here, it's easy to bring in other quotes from the text to say that she is now in a poorhouse and that she had to get up very early. The student can then go back to the text to pick up other quotations to support their point.

Both writers focus on some of the problems of working as a teenager, although in Text A, those problems are relatively minor and in Text B, they are very serious. In Text B, she cannot even find the words to describe "the pain and weariness" she feels. The way she describes the "weariness" of the work makes it sound as if it is not just tiring, but it completely exhausts her to such a point that she doesn't even know how to describe it. It is such hard work that it's not only left her drained and weak, but unable to work anymore. It is not a surprise to learn at the end of the text that she is "in a poorhouse" because of the "hardship and cruelty". The use of all of the descriptions in their abstract noun form ...

The student also notices that pain, weariness, hardship and cruelty are all abstract nouns. It's clearly something the writer is doing on purpose, since they could have written painful, weary, difficult, miserable or cruel instead, but it's not immediately clear why the writer needed to use the abstract noun form rather than adjectives. Here, it can be helpful to understand what the technique does. Abstract nouns are qualities or ideas. Adjectives are emotions. They come and go. After a bit of thinking, the abstract nouns here exist in their own right, as if they are independent of her, rather than just some feeling or sensation she has. Once they've thought this idea through, they are ready to try to explain.

It is such hard work that it's not only left her drained and weak, but unable to work anymore. It is not a surprise to learn at the end of the text that she is "in a poorhouse" because of the "hardship and cruelty". The use of all of the descriptions in their abstract noun form rather than adjectives helps the reader realise that they are bigger than just feelings, they are ideas. They go beyond just her and seem like insurmountable obstacles rather than just a feeling to deal with. When we're weary, we know it won't last forever, but when we're facing 'weariness', it is a thing in its own right, not something that comes and goes.

Noticing these small aspects of language and **why the writer has used them** is insightful in itself. Once you have explored one text, you can then **link up to the second**.

Both writers focus on some of the problems of working as a teenager, although in Text A, those problems are relatively minor and in Text

B, they are very serious. In Text B, she cannot even find the words to describe "the pain and weariness" she feels. The way she describes the "weariness" of the work makes it sound as if it is not just tiring, but it completely exhausts her to such a point that she doesn't even know how to describe it. It is such hard work that it's not only left her drained and weak, but unable to work anymore. It is not a surprise to learn at the end of the text that she is "in a poorhouse" because of the "hardship and cruelty". The use of all of the descriptions in their abstract noun form rather than adjectives helps the reader realise that they are bigger than just feelings, they are ideas. They go beyond just her and seem like insurmountable obstacles rather than just a feeling to deal with. When we're weary, we know it won't last forever, but when we're facing 'weariness', it is a thing in its own right not something that comes and goes and they are things that affect a lot of other "doffers". However in Text A, the writer admits that it was "an early start" but that it wasn't "bad work" which sounds much, much less of a challenge. Although she says it's "no wonder" she found school "so exhausting", it is just mentioned very fleetingly and the balance of positives seems to have been worth doing the job for. Also, she chose to work for pocket money so she could buy "posters" and "magazines", whereas the writer in Text A seems to have had little choice about working, and even then, she didn't earn enough for the vital "stays" that would make work less painful.

~ Reading skills: Making critical comparisons ~

Because this is such a long and developed paragraph, there would be no need to attempt three paragraphs like this. Writing in detail has its costs, which is why it's so important to focus on the right quotes.

Remember, you are being assessed on two strands: your ability to compare <u>and</u> your ability to comment on techniques. You can look back at how students write about language techniques to ensure you understand what **basic**, **straightforward**, **successful** or **skilful** comments look like at each level.

Teachers are also looking for **basic**, **straightforward**, **successful** or **skilful** comparisons.

Basic comparisons

Basic comparisons or cross-references are usually seen where students write one paragraph or sentence that is loosely on the topic, simply identifying how the writer feels about the topic, and then another linked very loosely. This usually says the second writer either feels exactly the same or feels the opposite. It may not even be about the same subject or linked in any way.

In Text A, the writer enjoys going to work and she loves being out in the early morning. She says "racing to catch up if we'd left a couple of pints at the bottom of a long driveway." This tells us that they were hurrying to get the work done so they could enjoy the morning.

On the other hand, in Text B, the writer does not enjoy going to work. She says she has been working "since I was six" which tells us she has been working a really long time as she is twenty-three and she has been working for seventeen years. She is very tired of going to work and getting up early.

Often at this level, the quotes don't really support what the student says and there may be some misunderstanding. They may paraphrase what the text says, and the quotes don't really match each other at all.

Straightforward comparisons

Straightforward comparisons are usually seen where there is an attempt to link the obvious ideas together. They may spot language or structural features and ideas and try to say things about them.

In Text A, the writer's perspective is that work is exhausting but that it gave her money to buy things that she wanted. For example she uses an example and a rule of three to say that she bought "a couple of magazines, a couple of music singles or a poster of my favourite bands" which shows us that she could use the money to buy things. In Text B, the writer's perspective is that work is very cruel and hard and that she is very tired. She doesn't even get enough money to buy the things she needs like "stays" to keep her back straight and they can be sacked for being slow. She only uses one example and no rule of three whereas Text A uses rule of three. This shows that both texts get some money for working but the first writer only thinks working is exhausting whereas the second writer thinks work is cruel.

Here, they have picked up an obvious point that both writers can either buy things they need or want, or not. There is some understanding of the idea in both. The references do support the comments but the identification of techniques is basic and only shows a little understanding of why the writer would use examples. The student knows that there are examples, but not why they have been used. They are trying to compare, and the little summary sentence at the end and at the beginning brings both together.

Successful comparisons

To make a **successful** comparison, you need to use linked quotations. You would also need to show a sound understanding of the techniques the writers have used and why they have used them.

In Text A, the only fault the writer finds with work is "the early start" which meant she found school "exhausting". She enjoyed the early mornings in the summer and says it has left her as "an early bird rather than a night owl" which shows that she feels her work as a teenager changed how she was as an adult. In Text B however, the writer feels that starting at 5am and finishing at 9pm has left her feeling that "the hardship and cruelty" were "too much to carry" showing that she feels work has broken her, mainly because it caused her severe suffering. In Text A, work prepared her for the future and in Text B, work destroyed her body so she did not have a future and is in "the poorhouse".

This answer has a solid comparison of the ideas in both texts, but does not explain how the writers use techniques. Because this strand is so important, it's really helpful to stop at the end of each paragraph and ask yourself if you have written about what techniques the writers are using, and why.

For instance, both quotes the student has picked out use language figuratively to compare their experiences. Adding a sentence to explain this, either for each text or as a summary can help.

In Text A, the only fault the writer finds with work is "the early start" which meant she found school "exhausting". She enjoyed the early mornings in the summer and says it has left her as "an early bird rather than a night owl" which shows that she feels her work as a teenager changed how she was as an adult. **The use of the clichéd metaphors helps us understand how she was like those birds getting the cream off the milk, rather than staying up late. It helps us understand how she felt getting up early gave her an advantage over "the night owls".** In Text B however, the writer feels that starting at 5am and finishing at 9pm has left her feeling that "the hardship and cruelty" were "too much to carry" showing that she feels work has broken her, mainly because it caused her severe suffering. **The writer also uses a figurative image of her "carrying" "hardship and cruelty" to show the idea that she felt crushed by the weight of work, that she couldn't bear it.** In Text A, work prepared her for the future and in Text B, work destroyed her body so she did not have a future and is in "the poorhouse".

Adding those extra sentences helps ensure you write skilfully.

Skilful comparisons

To write **skilfully**, you need to show that you can pick out insightful points of comparison and you can be detailed and perceptive when discussing ideas and perspectives.

What helps here is to think of the **overall perspective** of both passages based on the evidence. Once you have your long list, **pick out the key evidence** from both passages that seems to be the most essential, the most crucial. What is the one quote that says it all? That choice will be very personal to you, but for this student, the "real appreciation" of work, being "proud" of how hard she worked contrasts with the fact that in Text B, the writer feels that work has broken her, that it is "too much to carry". Which quote is the very best at showing their thoughts? Then compare this with the most essential quote from the other passage.

To create an insightful comparison depends on the quality of your quotation. Go back to your evidence and try to get to the central idea that underpins the whole passage. Write your first sentence to summarise that link between the two perspectives.

Both writers build up to a final revelation about their views of working. In Text A, the writer says she now has a "real appreciation" of work as a result of working when she was a teenager, that she is "proud" of how hard she worked whereas in Text B, the writer ends with the statement that "the hardship and cruelty" is too much to carry. Taylor focuses on the positives, and even though she could have focused on the dark nights, the early starts, the fact that school is "exhausting", the fact she needed two pairs of gloves and that in winter, the weather forced them to take longer in cold and dark conditions, she focuses instead on the positives, the small luxuries she can then afford, which aren't very much really, a "couple of magazines, a couple of music singles" or a "poster" aren't expensive, but it gave her some independence despite the long hours she had to work for them. In fact, these things weren't the biggest gains she found from work, with the "early morning twilight", the foxes and the birds being described in most beautiful ways, and it is these things that have changed her perspective about life for good, with a "deep love" of those early summer mornings, where Ogden in Text B finds nothing of merit in any of her work, which is not surprising since she can't find the words to describe "the pain and weariness". All that work has left her with is an unsupportable burden and a future "in the poorhouse". Work, for Pamela Taylor, was clearly something of a challenge, yet she sees how it changed her forever, and she has a "real appreciation" for the lessons she has learned, whereas for Elizabeth Ogden, she realises how much work has damaged her, having stolen her health and left her with no way to support herself.

The difference between the previous example and the one you see here is that for a solid response, the answer is very systematic. It follows a pattern of picking out something from Text A, exploring the writer's language and ideas, then comparing that to Text B. It is methodical and thorough, never deviating from the paragraph plan. This answer is a **skilful** understanding of how the perspective in the texts differs. Everything they write is helping to explore the big ideas, the central view. It's all woven together.

Example responses and commentary

Response 1

In Text A the writer says she got her first job when she was twelve. A quote to show this is "By the time I was twelve, I got my first job working a milk round before school." The writer uses numbers and statistics to persuade us and convince us. In Text B however, the writer is twenty-three years old. She worked in a flax mill belonging to Mr Burke. "We spun the flax to turn it into linen." She was a little doffer. They did different jobs.

In Text A the writer says she went to work at 5am. "We were up at 5am". This means she was late for school and might mean she would get in trouble for working. The writer uses facts to engage us and to make us interested in her work. In Text B they are saying they are late for work and she would get in trouble. A quote to show this is "if we were late or if we were slow, we would get the strap." This is showing they didn't like to go to work late. She uses pronouns but Text A doesn't use pronouns.

In this response, the student has selected some basic details and identified some obvious techniques. There is some basic comment on the effect of the techniques but it is generalised and not relevant. There is also some inaccuracy, as the writer in Text A was not late for school, nor is there any evidence that they would get in trouble for working. Although there are similar details picked out and put side by side which might show the student is trying to compare, this is more of a simple cross-reference and there is no real attempt to compare the writers' varying perspectives about work. Although they mention the writer in Text B uses pronouns, it is incorrect that in Text A the writer doesn't use pronouns. Perhaps they mean to highlight the different use of "we" compared to "I" in the first text, but that is unclear.

Advice

To improve further, this student needs to:

- Pick out linked quotations.
- Attempt to explain what they show about the writer's perspective.
- Pick out relevant techniques.
- Explain the effects of the words they are focusing on.
- Attempt to explore the meaning of quotations using synonyms.

Response 2

Firstly, the writers both describe what the job is like as working as a teenager. In Text A, a quote for this is: 'Those jobs were much less strenuous'. This quote means the workers were having an easier time with some of their jobs. The word 'strenuous' is an adjective and means difficult, which tells us this job at the time was easier because it was 'much less strenuous'. However for Text B, a quote for this is 'it is often intolerable'. This quote means it was impossible and difficult for her job. In Text A, she could do the work and it wasn't too hard, but in Text B, it was almost too hard for her.

Secondly, the writers both describe what the work must have felt like as a teenager. In Text A, a quote for this is 'our work wasn't unrewarded though'. This quote means the work involved was paid with money and these workers would have been happy. The adjective 'unrewarded' suggests they have made a lot of progress in their work and people recognized how much work they had done. For Text B, a quote for this is' I've been living in the poorhouse the last year because I cannot work'. This quote means she physically couldn't do anything. She has no rewards for how hard she has worked.

Thirdly, the writers both describe what had happened to the workers as teenagers. In Text A, a quote for this is, 'we definitely felt appreciated'. This quote means the workers are getting nice comments from different people. The word 'definitely' suggests they did get replies and comments and they would feel welcomed for their job. For Text B, a quote for this is 'many of us are half-starved', this means these workers haven't had any food or water.

The details chosen by this student are appropriate and relate to their experience of work. The student identifies some techniques but doesn't show any attempt to explain why these are important or how the words impact on our understanding. They attempt to compare the workers' perspectives, comparing how in Text A, they felt rewarded and appreciated but in Text B, they didn't feel the same, although this is not explored fully. There are some straightforward comments on perspective, that they felt 'welcomed' but some of the comments on the second text are not explored in the same detail.

Advice

To improve further, this student needs to:

- Explain why the techniques have been chosen and what they add to the writing.
- Explain what the writer's perspective is, but how the techniques help share that perspective.
- Focus equally on the second text.
- Make a summary statement to bring the two points together.

Response 3

Throughout the two passages it is clear that in both of the workplaces, there are times where you can get harmed and pain and suffering is involved. In passage A we are told that if they were to forget their gloves, they'd, "leave skin on bottles", but in passage B, if they were to try and stop the machines, some have ended up with, "broken hands or feet." Clearly, the consequences of work are much more severe in passage B, especially since there didn't seem to be any other way to work quicker, whereas in passage A, all they needed were a pair of gloves. There were no consequences if they had to work slower other than finishing later, and although the icy mornings could have ended with a "ticket to the hospital", the way the writer describes this with the euphemistic language to make it sound like a day-trip or a holiday, we can imagine the damage falling on smashed glass could do. In passage B, however, the writer is factual when she says they have "broken their hands or feet" or "lost fingers", which makes it sound like it's just part of the job. In passage A, she uses euphemism to avoid explaining the risks of the job and in passage B, she clearly explains the risks in a factual way as if it is just part of their job.

In the two passages we learn that there are times when the work gets hard but things were always easier when people worked as a team and helped each other. From passage A we learn that in the grocers, "Everybody had their role and the shop ran smoothly." We learn that is everyone does their assigned job correctly without problems then there will be fewer issues. In passage B the workers, "worked in link...so that we wouldn't get caught out." In passage A the workers each have a rota and assigned jobs that is done correctly, they would avoid the problematic consequences. However in passage B, they are forced to "work in link" simply to avoid punishment. There's no sense in passage A that they felt they had to work together other than for the pride of having done the job properly, whereas in passage B, they were watchful and wary. In passage A, she is observational: "Everybody" and she is more detached perhaps because she is less invested in her work whereas in passage B, she uses personal pronouns to make it sound as if "we" needed to work together against "the overlookers" which makes her sound more emotional about having to work together which is not surprising considering what the overlookers do if they catch them out.

In this response, there is a sound understanding of the writers' perspectives about work. The student has identified techniques used by the writer and tried to compare these. At the end of the second paragraph, there is a successful comparison of the different viewpoints explaining how and why they differ. There is accurate identification by the end of the different perspectives of the two writers. The details used are relevant, using these to build an argument.

Advice

To improve further, this student needs to:

- Try to be developed and insightful when making comments by exploring the subtle details.
- Explore the way the writers' techniques convey their perspective.

Response 4

A clear difference between the two teenagers' perspectives on work, is the varying difficulty. Though Pamela Taylor, from Text A, finds some of her jobs 'so exhausting', the jobs appear to be rather laid back as implied by the activities that she could get up to, while 'at 5a.m.' in her milk delivery job, for example. Implications of the easy-going journeys past driveways (where she would deliver milk), is from her being able to take in the 'blue skies' and 'morning twilight'. With the use of adjectives, we can see that she has the time to contemplate just how calm and beautiful her surroundings were. On the contrary, Elizabeth Ogden has the complete opposite perspective on her factory shown by how she was 'always frightened of getting the strap or not getting paid'. The usage of a clear, declarative statement shows a serious mood and as a result, conveys a sense of the grim and sombre experiences in the 'prison-like' work-place. In Text A, the writer describes the environment to show how work helped her appreciate the world in different ways and gave her a new outlook, whereas in Text B, the writer's description of the 'infernal' surroundings intensifies our understanding of what a hellish place it really was.

The dissimilar freedom of the girls is shown further through the texts. In Text A, it says 'We'd hang out on Friday and Saturday nights too', while in Text B, it states that 'the mill gates are locked, you cannot come or go.' Pamela is able to spend her free-time enjoying the company of her friends (as implied by hanging out), and through the colloquial language of 'We'd', 'hang out' and 'too', through her eyes it is seems like a casual and quite interesting experience, and as though she is used to such comfortable experiences. However, in the case of Elizabeth, the harsh, factual tone of the sentence about not being allowed to leave the factory shows such a cruel experience of work.

The misfortune of the factory-worker, is continued with her not nearly having enough to survive. 'The food is very ordinary and not plentiful' and many of the workers 'are half-starved', conveying the eternal sense of hardship. A combination of the short sentences and basic language, here, can be seen to emulate the lack of the necessities and just how little she receives for her work. On the other hand, Text A's job gave her enough 'every week to buy a couple of magazines, a couple of music singles' or a poster of' her 'favourite bands', making her seem so much more lucky, because she gets enough money for pleasurable items. Through the use of listing, the complexity of her job is emphasised, and it is as though she has a completely contrasting fortune compared with Elizabeth. In Text B, her use of brief, hard, simple sentences emphasises how little work provided for her, whereas in Text A, the writer's use of listing emphasises how much work provided, not just in terms of the trivial things she could buy but how it allowed her to make friends. The list and long sentences emphasise just how much work gave her, leaving her with a 'real appreciation' of work.

This answer is both developed and insightful. It has a strong focus on comparison and uses evidence from the text to build a case to support their thoughts. There is insightful understanding of the way the writers use sentences to convey their perspective, explaining nicely how this contributes to meaning.

Summary

- Remember you need to do both comparison **and** discussion of writers' techniques.

- A good answer starts with good evidence.

- Use a highlighter to scan the text to make a broad selection before narrowing down using close reading skills to focus on a more limited range of details. Use two different colours of highlighter to mark positive and negative perspectives.

- Try to consider the big feelings or views, then identify which quotations support that.

- Try to consider which quote would be the 'one' quote that summarises the perspective of the writer, and make sure you include it in your response.

- Be precise with your quotations and focus in on the key words of each detail.

- Start each paragraph or section with an overview that states the main similarity or difference, and come back to that statement at the end of each paragraph or section as well.

- When you think about what techniques the writer has used, try to think about why they needed that particular one to convey that particular idea.

~ Making a personal critical response to texts ~

In your exam, you will be asked to write some longer responses to the texts that you are given. Usually, these will ask you to write for between 15-25 minutes. They ask you to make an argument to agree or disagree with a statement in the question. These questions focus on one text.

What you are being tested on

- Can you **identify and explain** the key ideas in the text?
- Can you **write a short essay** focusing on a given theme or idea?
- Can you **use evidence from the text** to justify your point of view?
- Do you understand the **writer's techniques and purpose**?
- Can you **explain the effects** of the writer's choices?

Sample task

Text C shows how writers can create a sense of panic and fear. The part of the story, where the candles go out is terrifying and the narrator is right to panic.

How far do you agree with this statement?

In your answer, you could:

- consider your own impressions of the narrator's reaction to the events that happen
- evaluate how successfully the writer presents a sense of panic
- support your response with quotations from the text.

About the question

If the question specifies lines that you must base your answer on, make sure you mark these off on the text.

You will be given a statement about the extract that you have read. Sometimes, there have been two parts to the statement. It is helpful when there are two parts because it gives you a simple structure for your essay: two paragraphs or sections on the first part, and two paragraphs or sections for the second. Other responses just focus on one single aspect and it is up to you to figure out your basic points and a structure for what you want to say.

That means for this example, you could spend two paragraphs exploring the idea that the passage is terrifying and two paragraphs exploring the idea that the narrator is right to panic.

You can use the words of the statement to help you start your paragraphs off and help you structure your plan. The key words in the statement will also help you find parts of the text to explore. Your first task is to find out exactly what relates to the question from the passage.

Understanding how you are marked

There are four components that are assessed as part of your response.

1. Respond to the statement.
2. Find evidence to help support your response.
3. Discuss the techniques used by the writer.
4. Evaluate the impact of these techniques on the reader.

If you do not write about all of these, you cannot access all the marks available.

Like other questions, your comments and your understanding of techniques is **basic**, **straightforward**, **successful** or **skilful**.

How that looks in students' responses:

	Comment	and	Understanding of Technique
Basic response	Basic awareness of ideas, meaning and effect		Basic identification of **what** the writer is doing
Straightforward response	Some understanding of ideas, meaning and effect		Accurate identification of **what** the writer is doing
Successful response	Sound understanding of ideas, meaning and effect		Accurate identification of **what** the writer is doing and **what**
Skilful response	Insightful or developed understanding of ideas, meaning and effect		Insightful or developed understanding of **what** the writer is doing and **what**

How to improve your answer

Key steps:

- Before you answer this question, **mark off the lines** that the question refers to if necessary.
- **Identify the key words** in the statement.

- Make sure you **discuss the whole statement**, especially if there is more than one aspect of it.

- Make sure you **cover both the writer's techniques and ideas**, as well as their effect.

- Use **different coloured highlighters** for each focus point to identify quotes that will go in each part of your essay, or for positive/negative thoughts and feelings.

- **Scan through** the text and make a broad selection of evidence.

- **Close read** your broad selection and make a more careful choice.

- Try to **aim for between 4 and 8 main quotes** for the whole essay.

Remember, when scanning and highlighting, you don't need to be precise. You just want to find the parts of the text that you **may** use eventually, before narrowing down. You may also find that some quotes would fit in both sections.

Terrifying	Right to Panic?
echoing of the stir and crackling of the fire The shadow in the corner at the end in particular had an odd suggestion of a lurking, living thing, that comes so easily in silence and solitude after midnight	I walked with a candle into it, and satisfied myself that there was nothing there. to my reason there was no cause for the condition. My mind, however, was perfectly clear. I decided that nothing supernatural could happen.

suddenly went out, and the black shadow sprang back to its place	It occurred to me that when the ghost came, I could warn him not to trip over them.
something seemed to blink on the wall before me	I walked across the room in a leisurely manner
I saw the candle in the right sconce of one of the mirrors wink and go right out,	"Odd!" I said. "Did I do that myself?"
There was no mistake about it. The flame vanished, as if the wicks had been suddenly nipped between a finger and thumb,	I saw the candle in the right sconce of one of the mirrors wink and go right out,

Once you have scanned and highlighted directly on the passage, you should then use close reading skills to narrow down. You will be using your appraisal skills to find the most useful quotations for your short list.

   Once you have done this, then appraise your quotations. You will need to think over and justify your choices as you weigh up their value.

Terrifying	Right to Panic?
suddenly went out, and the black shadow **sprang back** to its place	**satisfied myself that there was nothing there**.
something seemed to blink on the wall before me	I **decided** that nothing supernatural could happen.

I **saw** the candle in the right sconce of one of the mirrors wink and go right out,	It occurred to me that when the ghost came, I could warn him not to trip over them.
There was no mistake about it. The flame **vanished, as if the wicks had been suddenly nipped between a finger and thumb,**	I walked across the room in a leisurely manner "Odd!" I said. **"Did I do that myself?"** I **saw** the candle in the right sconce of one of the mirrors wink and go right out,

As you can see here, the student has cut down on some of the long list and has highlighted eight quotes that they want to use across the whole answer. They also have one that goes across both aspects of the essay.

Once you have these, you are ready to start writing.

Remember as you start that you can agree or disagree, or agree a little, or disagree a little. There is no 'right' answer about how true these statements are. The key skill assessed in this question is evaluation, not whether you can make an argument or not.

So what does evaluation of an idea or a technique look like?

Basic evaluation

The most basic evaluation is **basic, limited or undeveloped.** Usually students may very simply **identify what** the technique is:

> I completely agree with what the student has said. The room is terrifying. "It was after midnight that the candle in the alcove suddenly went out." *This would be scary and make the man feel like something bad was going to happen. The man must have been very frightened.* **The word "suddenly" means it happened quickly.**

Straightforward evaluation

An improvement on this is where evaluation is **straightforward or valid.** This often means that the evaluation is either putting the quotation into your own words but not in context.

It may also mean that you have got the right idea behind the passage but the ideas you have don't come from the evidence that you have selected. Your quotes and your comments don't match. Your comment is right, just not about the right part of the text.

It may mean that you know **what** the writer is doing but don't really explain **why**. Or you may explain **why** but it is not really the effect that the words have.

Students may write things like:

> I completely agree with what the student has said because towards the end of the text, **there is a simile** *that makes it sound as if candles were put out by a human* "as if the wicks had been suddenly

nipped between a finger and thumb" so in this respect the narrator is definitely right to start panicking. I don't agree that he is right to start panicking because there were a lot of candles "at least seventeen candles" *so it suggests there is a lot of light and it's only one or two shadows that have come back.*

Here, the student knows what the writer has done and has some understanding why they might have done that.

Successful evaluation

To improve further, evaluation is **successful** in relation to the techniques the writer is using and/or the ideas in the passage.

Students may write things like:

I agree with this statement as the writer creates an atmosphere of terror in the shadows, stating "one of the shadows had an odd suggestion of a lurking, living thing" which not only makes it sound as if it is alive, but the word "lurking" gives us the idea that the shadow is just waiting for the right moment, as if it is just hanging around up to no good.

This shows a clear understanding of the idea in the word "lurking" and what it suggests.

Students at this level may also show a **sound** understanding of the writer's techniques, identifying **what** the writer is doing and understanding **why** they are doing it. What they say is plausible, rooted in the evidence and thoughtful.

Skilful evaluation

The best responses are **skilled** and **developed** in relation to evaluating ideas and/or techniques. They really understand what the writer is trying to do, or what the idea is behind the text. They appreciate the writer's craft and truly understand the effect.

You may also understand that a technique used by the writer could have a variety of effects.

An example of these kinds of responses might be:

Superficially, there is little that is terrifying about darkness and a few shadows, as the narrator points out. He tries to use 'reason' to banish his fears, saying 'there was no cause' for his nervous tension and acknowledging that it is all in his mind. He even jokes about the number of candles he's put around the room, saying 'when the ghost came, I could warn him not to trip over them'. It's in this joke, however, that we see the narrator has already determined there will be a ghost: it's 'when' and not 'if' the ghost arrives. There is no speculation about the ghost, and although he's already decided he's being ridiculous, that it is more likely to be a human trick than a ghost by putting out his 'revolver' and a 'barricade' that would be no challenge for a truly supernatural being, he is already determined by that point that the ghost will appear and his language betrays him. Although the narrator becomes highly agitated, we can see that despite his attempts to convince himself using 'systematic evaluation' and 'reason' that 'something' would happen and we begin to see that his terrors are all in his mind. For this reason, the passage is not that terrifying: we see a man at the mercy of his irrational fears. This also means that there is little reason to panic: indeed, some might argue that it is panic that causes him to feel terrified. He even admits there may be a strong 'draught'.

On the other hand, however, by the end of the passage, with the way the darkness seems to be winning the battle and putting out the candles, it is the simile at the end that works to persuade both us and the narrator that this is not a draught at all, as the wicks are not 'glowing' or 'smoking' as they would be if they had been blown out, but they are 'black' as if they have been put out 'between a finger and a thumb'. Still, it is only a simile, just a way to describe how they looked, not a definitive statement that they could only have been put out like that, and we are left knowing there are still lots of candles and a fire which was 'burning well', meaning that the narrator has no real need to panic at all.

In this partial response, the student is **developed** in their argument that there is no real reason to panic and also that the passage is not really that terrifying. They're exploring in a number of different ways. They show they truly understand the fact that the final image is just a comparison and that there may be other reasons for the candles having gone out. They use evidence to make their argument, embedding their quotations in the passage as a way to argue a case.

Example responses and commentary

Response 1

I agree fully with this statement. The story is terrifying. It's terrifying when the candles go out and it hooks the reader making them intrigued about what will happen next. The writer says 'suddenly' which makes it seem like the narrator is in a rush.

I also agree that the narrator is panicking. "My first match would not strike". This shows he is scared and terrified. It's no wonder he panics as anyone would with the candles blowing out like that.

In this response, the student has a basic response to the statement, saying that they 'agree fully'. They refer to some simple details and have some basic evaluation of those details. They have a simple awareness that 'suddenly' was chosen on purpose; it is not, however, the narrator being in a rush but the candles going out that is sudden. They refer to both parts of the statement and write an undeveloped evaluation related to the narrator panicking.

Advice

To improve further, the student needs to:

- Identify the writer's techniques.
- Pick out quotations that better support the statement.
- Explain what the words tell us in relation to the statement.

Response 2

I agree with the student's statement that the events are terrifying because the description of the room and the darkness makes me feel on edge and nervous that something might happen. This is shown in the quote "the shadow in the corner at the end in particular had an odd suggestion of a lurking, living thing". The writer uses alliteration to show the shadow seems to be alive, suggesting that they are supernatural and horrifying. This is further proven by the description that the "black shadow sprang back". The use of this personification shows the shadow is terrifying and menacing and the word "sprang" makes it sound startling.

I also agree with the student's response as the narrator is right to panic as it is clear he won't be able to win against all the shadows and the blackness. The narrator is panicking and the use of the quote "there was no mistake about it" emphasises the fact that he is not being tricked. This is for real. This is also shown by the quote "the flame vanished". The verb "vanished" makes it sound like the flame disappeared. However the narrator is also brave because he is trying to relight the candles. This is shown when it says "I walked back, relit one" which makes it sound like he is fighting back.

This student has some response to both parts of the statement and they have picked out some appropriate details that relate to the scene being terrifying or the narrator panicking. They have correctly identified alliteration and a verb, but they have no real understanding of why alliteration or a verb are relevant.

Advice

To improve further, the student needs to:

- Match quotes up more carefully with the statement.
- Identify what techniques the writer has used specifically for a purpose.
- Explain what the writer's purpose is.
- Comment on the meaning of the words used and the ideas they convey.

Response 3

I agree to some extent that the story is terrifying as it seems like the writer really brings the shadows to life saying they had an "odd suggestion of a living, lurking thing" where the present participle verbs really bring the shadow to life and gives them movement and motion, and the word "lurking" suggests they are up to no good, giving them a menacing quality. Despite that, however, the writer then goes on to tell us that the narrator came to the conclusion that "there was nothing there" so we know he can't really come to any harm. The narrator tells us repeatedly that "there was no cause for the condition", that "nothing supernatural could happen" and "there was nothing there" so that we too are reassured nobody is hiding in the shadows. Although it is not particularly terrifying that the candles go out, the writer makes it terrifying by the end where they say the candles went out "as if nipped between a finger and thumb" which suggests that they have not just been blown out. Since nobody has put them out and they haven't been blown out, what else could it be? That is terrifying as it can only be something supernatural.

At first the narrator seems to be changing between confident and nervous. He does lots of things to make himself feel safe, like putting up a barricade and getting out his revolver, and he realises it's just the "sombre reds and blacks of the room" that are making him feel nervous. He is joking that the ghost might need to be warned not to trip over the candlesticks but then he seems to question himself, "Did I do that myself?" which suggests he knows he didn't put the candle out, but he can't quite believe someone or something else might have done it. This makes him panic especially when he sees the other candles go out right before his eyes.

In this response, the candidate has successfully responded to the statement and has picked out a number of relevant details that support what they are saying. They have identified what the writer is doing and why they have used language features such as present participles. They have made sound comments on the meaning of words and phrases, picking out the key ideas and feelings behind it.

Advice

To improve further, the student needs to:

- Make their comments more detailed.
- Explore the ideas expressed.
- Explore the purpose and effect of the writer's techniques.

Response 4

The student is correct to some degree that the story is frightening, although the threat is largely psychological rather than physical. The narrator has gone to great lengths to show there is no possibility of human intervention, having locked the door and checked all the alcoves. He is satisfied that there is no way anybody is hiding having "satisfied" himself that "nothing" was lurking in the shadows. That said, he still has out a "barricade" and a "revolver" suggesting he thinks someone playing a prank is more likely than supernatural events. There is nothing particularly terrifying about candles blowing out in themselves, but it is the way the "suddenly went out" just "after midnight" that creates the first psychological terror: we associate midnight with 'the witching hour', the time when spirits are free to do as they like. Although a rational person as the narrator seems to be would not be normally influenced by such myths, he has already acknowledged the "dim" room "troubled" him, suggesting he can't put the eerie qualities of the shadows in the room to one side. The way the narrator keeps mentioning the shadows adds to the sense of threat that they give, often being personified right from the opening of the text, bringing them to life. Ironically, the shadows are only created because of the light, it is the fire that "kept the shadows perpetually shifting and stirring". His attempts to keep the light alive are what give the shadows life as well. We can see that there is nothing particularly terrifying about the room, even when one of the candles goes out as he is looking directly at it. It is the momentum of all these things, the darkness, the shadows, the legends, the time of night, the "sombre reds and blacks" and the way he doesn't notice the first candle going out but the others then seem to go out in quick succession, including two that go out whilst he is looking at them that creates the psychological terror of the room and we are left in no doubt that despite our best efforts, we too would not fail to be influenced by the spooky qualities of the room, especially as the candles begin to go out in such an unnatural way.

As to whether the narrator is right to panic, one could argue that whilst his panic is natural because the situation is so psychologically terrifying, his panic is misplaced. First, there is a large fire, large enough to "keep the shadows perpetually shifting and stirring". The description of perpetual motion is interesting because it suggests an everlasting or inextinguishable quality, as if it can't be put out. For candles to go out is one thing but the fire will still bring enough light to the room that he won't be left in complete darkness. Not only that, he also acknowledged at the beginning that the events in the room were largely accidental, with no explanation of how the duke had died. It was undoubtedly his panic that caused that. If the threat is human (unlikely after his extensive checks) then he has a revolver, and if the threat is supernatural, it won't have the physical power to do anything to him. Darkness and shadows can't literally kill anyone, despite what mystery stories and horror films suggest. We might even question whether he is indeed panicking. He seems nervous, and admits he was filled with "considerable nervous tension" but at the same time, he's trying to reason that a "draught" caused the candles to go out, and the simile at the end "as if nipped between a finger and thumb" is only that: a comparison to help us understand how the candle seemed to have gone out. It gives the air of some kind of ghostly intervention, but at the same time, it is just a simile designed to help us understand. There is no evidence that he actually believes it is anything other than a "draught", mysterious as it is.

This answer is both developed and thought-provoking. It has a strong focus on the statement and uses evidence from the text to build a case to justify their beliefs. There is an insightful understanding of the idea behind "perpetually" and behind the simile at the end that shows thoughtful understanding of both the ideas and the reasons why the writer may have used these techniques.

Summary

- If the question asks you to refer to specific lines, put a box around them and take your quotes from those lines.

- Respond to the statement **and** discuss of writers' techniques.

- Start with good evidence.

- Scan the text and use a highlighter to make a long list of quotes.

- When you have made a long list, then use close reading to focus in on a selective range.

- Consider the overarching feelings or views, then identify which quotations support that.

- If the statement you are given to respond to has different components, make sure you explore each aspect in detail.

- Be precise with your quotations and focus in on the key words.

- Pay attention to your time management.

- Start each paragraph or section with a sentence that relates to the statement you have been given, and come back to that at the end of each paragraph.

- When you think about what techniques the writer has used, try to think about why they needed that particular one to convey that particular idea.

Section 2: Writing skills

~ Quality of language ~

No matter what you are asked to write, the main thing that matters when you write is your **quality of language**. You don't have to have a genius level of vocabulary to get good grades. In fact, the main thing to do is avoid the things that just don't work. Usually, it's where you've put in a simile that is clichéd, used some alliteration that just doesn't go or you've used words wrongly. It's so easy to use words wrongly or to make mistakes because you're trying too hard.

Sample task

Write a description of a frightening place

HOW TO IMPROVE YOUR ANSWER

Basic responses just use **simple vocabulary** with **some occasional similes** or **metaphors**.

I went into the room and closed the door. A shadow jumped out like a tiger on its prey. I locked the door. Then I went over to the window and shut the curtains. I was afraid and when I looked in the mirror I was as white as a sheet. I thought I saw a ghost looking at me.

Writing like this is not very interesting.

Writing that is slightly better than this may put in **some straightforward words on purpose**. Students start to use **adjectives** and **adverbs** to add some colour and detail to their writing.

I went into the room and closed the door **carefully** behind me. A **deep, black** shadow jumped out like a tiger on its prey. I **confidently** locked the door. Then I went over to the window and shut the **large, velvet** curtains. I was afraid and when I looked in the mirror, I thought I saw a ghost looking at me.

This writing has some words that the student has chosen on purpose. They seem a little functional and repetitive, as they always write two adjectives in a list and they're not particularly interesting words. They don't seem to be there for any reason than the student knew they really should try to use some more adjectives. 'Carefully' is the nicest of all of those choices because it tells us something about the narrator. 'Confidently' is less effective because it's like the narrator has changed his feelings within one second. But it is still chosen for effect, even if it doesn't work very well.

Some of the vocabulary for students who write like this will be a bit stiff and unnatural. It is very clearly there to describe or add to the story, but it doesn't quite work.

Some students assume that complicated vocabulary and lots of language features must be the key to success and use them whether or not they work or they make sense. The words themselves might be quite nice, but the ideas are not particularly convincing.

I **marched gingerly** into the room and closed the door **dependably** behind me. An **abyssal angry assured ebony** shadow flabbergasted me and I was aghast. I **confidently** locked the door. Then I went over to the window and shut the **gigantic, enormous, gargantuan, velvet** curtains. I was afraid and when I looked in the mirror, I thought I saw a spectral looking at me.

It's clear that this student has learned a lot of words, but they don't know how to use them properly or even seem to understand their meaning. Marching, for instance, is never done 'gingerly' because marching is confident and 'gingerly' means with care and anxiety. Can you be both confident and anxious? They've also used some alliteration without thinking about why or what the effect should be. The word 'spectral' is used wrongly and should be 'spectre'. Writing like this certainly shows that the student is picking words on purpose, but it does not show they are using words well.

Writing that is better than this has some vocabulary that is **clearly chosen for effect** and it's **successful**.

I entered the room and closed the door **deliberately** behind me, making sure it clicked shut. The room was filled with shadows of every kind and shade. I **confidently** locked the door. Then I went over to the window and shut the **large, velvet** curtains. I was afraid and when I looked in the mirror, I thought I saw a ghost looking at me.

In this version, the vocabulary works. 'Deliberately' is a good choice because it shows the careful actions of the narrator. They've also added a little bit of detail afterwards to develop their ideas. After this, it has a nice explanation of the kind of shadows in the room, and a bit of detail. The writing is not perfect: 'confidently' still doesn't match the mood of the narrator, but the writing is all clear and interesting.

To improve further, students need to start doing some of the things that seem almost more like technical accuracy. There are **skilful language choices for effect** and the language features work well.

> I entered the room and closed the door **deliberately** behind me, hearing the handle click shut. The room was **a jungle of overgrown shadows of every kind and every shade**. I knew they were only shadows, but even so, I felt **uneasy and unsure**. I locked the door, knowing I was imprisoning myself with these monsters. The windows were **framed** by heavy velvet curtains, not yet closed against the darkness outside. As I moved, I caught myself in a mirror, startled.

Here, the student is beginning to use **patterning**. This is where you use repetition or similarities of words to create word patterns in an almost poetic way. It starts to contribute to what is considered 'sophisticated' language and vocabulary use. So we see the repetition of 'every kind and every shade'. It is not just about the use of the word 'every' but also how it is followed by a simple, monosyllabic word: 'kind' and 'shade'. They are also starting to use more interesting metaphors and similes, but these are contained within the sentence rather than growing beyond it. Some aspects of technical accuracy also help with the patterns here, such as the way the final sentence builds up to 'startled'. To improve further, the student will also be **expanding and developing those ideas**, **sustaining patterning**.

> I entered the room and closed the door **deliberately** behind me, hearing the handle click shut. The room before me was an **animated**

audience of bustling shadows: every size and every shape, caught up with a wind of interest and curiosity at the new arrival. For the first time, I felt as if I were there to entertain them, to fill their evening with tales and stories, rather than finally putting those tales and stories to rest. I locked the door with a certain irony: the dangers had always come from within. The windows were framed by heavy velvet curtains, **the night outside a bare stage, a drama yet to come to life, yet the glass reflected us, projecting me onto a makeshift cinema screen**. I closed them firmly: it was not as if I needed to add to the **drama**. It was only when I turned, startled, and caught myself in the mirror that I realised how on edge I was.

In this final version, we can see very clever patterning in 'animated audience' which plays on the sound of the words. The student starts with personifying the shadows as an audience and from there on, there are lots of words relating to the theatre. That idea from the second sentence runs right down through the paragraph. At this level, the student is not just playing with figurative language but they are also **developing and sustaining** it through several sentences. None of the words are complex or over-done. The images are both successful and skilful.

As you can see, the quality of your writing, the choices you make with vocabulary and imagery, enable your teacher to place your work within the mark scheme.

~ Writing articles ~

The type of text you are asked to write will have clear rules and conventions that you can use to make sure you have the right style and register. You will be able to use some of these to start your article off and to bring it to a close.

Sample task

'Children should be allowed to work: it helps them understand the real world, teaches them the value of money and prepares them for adult life.'

Write an article for a newspaper in which you explain your point of view on this statement.

How to improve your answer

Whether you are writing for a newspaper, a magazine or an online source, the first thing to remember is that articles have **headings or titles and subheadings**. It may sound obvious but this separates them from speeches and letters which do not.

There may also be a **summary strapline** underneath the title that explains what the article is about. This may range from a very simple one-line sentence to something that is two or three sentences long. The summary strapline is almost like a teaser for the article and you can use rhetorical questions or start with the counterarguments in order to entice your reader to continue.

Articles may also have a **third-person biography** of the writer as part of the summary introduction or at the end. Sometimes this can be as simple as *by Peter Osborn* or more detailed in some circumstances.

By framing your article with a heading, a summary strapline or opening paragraph and a concluding biography, you can certainly make a good start. If you are spending a lot of time trying to come up with a headline, however, you may want to leave some space and add it when you have finished.

Below, the student has started with a simple headline which they have then followed with a simple strapline explaining **what** the article is about and giving us a guide as to **who** the article is for (parents).

The value of work

How a job could prepare your teenager for life beyond school

If the student follows this with a simple opening paragraph that sets out the main problems in one sentence, poses some simple answers in response and then introduces the writer, it 'sounds' very much like article style.

The value of work

How a job could prepare your teenager for life beyond school

Many parents worry that their children have too much to do already, with GCSEs, school plays, sports, band practice and choir. But is there more to life than school? A job can often teach them the things that school can't: independence, working with adults and being proud of earning your own money. James Bishop explains his view about why a part-time job might just be the answer to your teenager's woes.

The difficulty of writing this first paragraph is that it needs you to predict what you are going to write later in the essay. For that, you must have a good plan.

You also need to think about your ending. This helps you be **developed** and **sustained**.

Newspaper articles, magazine articles and online articles have lots of stylistic features that you can use yourself that help to finish off your writing and bring it to a neat conclusion in a way that shows you can be consistent.

One of the main ways an article will do this is a **call to action** which invites you to do something. That could be a 'Call Crimestoppers Now on …' or a 'find out more about'. You could use **an imperative verb** - you can be encouraged to take action and do something, to read more, to find out more, to make an enquiry, to give a contribution, even to leave a comment. You could also use **conditionals** to do this, writing 'if you…' and 'you could…'.

You could also include a true **rhetorical question** to leave the reader something to reflect upon.

A **summary** is also a good way to end, where you will bring three or four of your key words together from each paragraph. You may want to use this as the paragraph just before your ending.

You can also **link** to other resources, other books, speeches, television programmes or YouTube channels to help people find out more information if they are interested.

Another way that articles end is often to give a **trailer** to something that will come next, introducing another writer's feature that will appear in the next edition.

Other articles, especially online or for magazines, will add a **third-person biography** as a way to end a piece as well, establishing authority to write about a subject. You only need one of these, so don't reuse it if you have included it at the beginning.

Finally, **linking back** to the opening can also help you bring your article to a neat conclusion.

Let's explore some of those things in relation to the opening written previously:

The value of work

How a job could prepare your teenager for life beyond school

Many parents worry that their children have too much to do already, with GCSEs, school plays, sports, band practice and choir. But is there more to life than school? A job can often teach them the things that school can't: independence, working with adults and being proud of earning your own money. James Bishop explains his view about why a part-time job might be just the answer to your teenager's woes.

* * * * *

Concluding paragraph:

As you can see, getting a job might be the answer you're looking for if you're worried your teenager isn't as self-reliant as they could be. Finding themselves in a world of adults needn't be intimidating and it can help them transition from a world of parents and teachers to a world of colleagues and equals. The added bonus of earning a bit of cash on the side is certainly not to be overlooked.

Call to action and author biography:

If you're interested in helping your teenager find a part-time job, keep an eye out for postings in your local papers, or check shop and restaurant windows. With the internet opening up a whole world of versatile jobs online, if your child has a particular skill, you may also find sites such as Freelancer or Fiverr of use.

James Bishop is a family psychologist. Find out more about James at BishopRelationshipGuidance.org

Using one or two of these devices appropriately to help finish off your article can help you show you truly understand the form you are writing.

~ Writing letters ~

Unlike magazines or news articles where you are writing for a largely unknown audience, letters are usually to a single reader or small group of readers.

Letters form part of a discussion rather than being a one-off event. They either establish the opening of a written dialogue or to continue one. That means you may need to explain who you are.

If the only thing you know about the style of letters is that they have an address, a 'Dear…' and finish with 'yours faithfully' or 'yours sincerely', you have some work to do!

There are lots of things to avoid. Starting with 'I am writing' is one of them. Of course you are writing. That is clear. You don't need to open by stating this. "I am writing to share my point of view on…" and "I am writing to argue that…" are very formulaic.

You may want to think about what would have prompted you to write a letter.

Sample task

'Students in secondary school leave with no idea about work. Schools should do more to allow their students to seek part-time work or to do work placements.'

Write a letter to your headteacher in which you explain your point of view on this statement.

Because so many letters in exams are directed to a formal, mostly unknown reader, this guidance will mainly focus on this readership. However, be prepared for your exam to ask you to write a less formal letter to your friend or to a known person with whom you have a closer relationship with.

So how can we make our text sound more like a letter other than just sticking a 'To Whom It May Concern' at the beginning and a 'Yours faithfully' at the end?

What even comes after the 'Dear'? Can you write 'To'? First names or surnames?

For our letter to our headteacher, which of openings on the next page work?

To Mr Scruton,	Are you writing a birthday card?
To Neil Scruton,	Are you writing a weird birthday card?
To Neil,	Is it your friend's birthday?
Dear Neil Scruton,	Are you writing junk mail or a scam email?
Dear Scruton,	Do you hold him in absolute disregard?
Neil,	Are you his really angry boss?
Dear Neil,	Are you his friendly boss or his client?

Dear Mr Neil Scruton,	Are you asking him for details of his bank account to scam him?
To Whom It May Concern	Can you not even be bothered to find out their name?
Dear Sir or Madam,	Are you politely not bothered to find out their name? Have you sent out thousands of the exact same letter?
Hi Neil,	Are you another headteacher asking your friend if he's free for golf on Saturday?

You can see how many ways there are to go wrong!

Dear Mr Scruton,

Lovely. Polite. If the first three words are that hard, you can see how hard it can be to get the tone right for the rest. Luckily it gets easier.

One way to start is stating what prompted you to write. Here, we can leave out the 'I am writing to you ...' and just get right to the reason. Why now? Why, of all the moments in all your days in all your life have you chosen this one to write?

Dear Mr Scruton,

I'm sure you are no doubt aware of the current media campaign to encourage students to seek out part-time employment so that they're better prepared for adult life...

Dear Mr Scruton,

Having read the school guidance for college applications, I thought the school may wish to consider...

As you can see, each of the openings above **explains the situation that prompted the letter** and **gives the topic** straight away. It's a good idea to start your letter by stating **what prompted you to write now**.

Sometimes, you may hear that you shouldn't use contractions such as "I'm" or "they're" but writing things out in full can seem cold, unfriendly and over-formal. It's a choice you'll have to make about your reader.

What is also a good thing to do in a letter is **explain who you are**.

Dear Mr Scruton,

I'm sure you are no doubt aware of the current media campaign to encourage students to seek out part-time employment so that they're better prepared for adult life. As a student in year 11, this could not be more timely for me...

Dear Mr Scruton,

Having read the school guidance for college applications, I thought the school may wish to consider my thoughts as a current year 11 student.

You don't have to say "I am a year 11 student in Mrs Belton's form and have studied at this school for 5 years..." or "My name is Philip Pirrip and I have been a student here at St Felicia's since my arrival in year 7". It doesn't have to be that obvious. Better writers will find subtle ways to state who they are and give the reader an insight without resorting to very obvious explanations.

Once you have set out your role, it is time to **explain why you are writing**. This should be clear but subtle. You don't want to waste your busy reader's time (even if they are a 'fake' reader and only your teacher marking your homework) by leaving that out. It also leaves your letter a bit adrift and directionless. You can also flatter your reader a little, but don't go over the top! First paragraphs of letters are no place to roll out the cheesy adjectives.

Dear Mr Scruton,

I'm sure you are no doubt aware of the current media campaign to encourage students to seek out part-time employment so that they're better prepared for adult life. As a student in year 11, this could not be more timely for me. I appreciate this is one concern of many for you as headteacher, but I hope you find some of my ideas worth considering.

Dear Mr Scruton,

Having read the school guidance for college applications, I thought the school may wish to consider my thoughts as a current year 11 student. Without wanting to take up too much of your time, I feel confident that some of my concerns are those shared by many of my classmates; as such, I hope they may be worth your thoughts as to how we could improve aspects relating to work experience.

What you don't want to do is lay on lots of schmooze. Here's an example that's so thick with schmooze that it's almost sickening…

My dearest Mr Scruton,

Without wanting to take up too much of your very precious and valuable time, I feel confident that some of my concerns are those shared by many of my classmates; as such, I very humbly hope they may be worth your most esteemed thoughts as to how we could improve aspects relating to work experience.

Leave out adjectives and adverbs from your introduction.
Overly critical letters also establish the wrong tone.

Neil,

You can't help but be aware of the current media campaign to encourage students to seek out part-time employment. Despite all the reasons, this school is ignoring our needs! We leave this school completely unprepared for adult life. As a student in year 11, this is severely jeopardising my chances of getting a place at college. I don't care how busy you are as headteacher, as this is a priority. It must change now!

Being rude or hostile doesn't get you anywhere. Leave out the negatives and the exclamation marks, don't insult your reader and remember that the purpose of your letter is to open a discussion. Establishing the right tone is vital.

Setting out **your motivation for writing**, an **integrated introduction about yourself** and why the topic is interesting to you, and **a polite statement of what you want the reader to do** can all help you frame your opening paragraph.

Like articles, many students are unsure as to how to finish. Also, like articles, you can adapt some of the ideas that may work, such as a **summary**, **a call to action** or **a way for them to find out more**. There are, however, many little flourishes you can add to the very final paragraph that add a touch of professionalism to your letter. Not all letters have to finish "yours sincerely" or "yours faithfully" - although "please accept my most respectful and distinguished gratitude in thanks for your esteemed consideration of my ideas" would certainly be too formal. Likewise, a "regards" or "best" can seem very cold.

At the same time, a letter such as this should be open to response, so leave something in there that makes it clear this is the opening of a written conversation.

As I am sure you appreciate, this is a topic which inspires me a great deal. Thank you for your time in considering my ideas. I very much look forward to your response.

Very cordially,

* * *

Thank you very much for having taken the time to consider my ideas;

I very much look forward to hearing from you.

With very best wishes,

* * *

If any of my ideas seem feasible, please don't hesitate to get in touch. I very much value the role of work experience and look forward to seeing how it can be enhanced in our school.

Respectfully yours,

These final endings are a step away from the robotic and thoughtless "yours sincerely" or "yours faithfully" and can add a polite, warm and respectful end to your letter. However, it's important to choose ones that are appropriate for a person you know in some capacity; they wouldn't all be as appropriate for an MP, a chair of the local council or a prime minister.

By starting and finishing your letters with some of these ideas, you can show that you really understand the style and purpose of this text type.

~ Writing speeches ~

Unlike articles and letters which are written forms of communication, a speech is designed to be delivered aloud.

Many have the idea that a speech explaining our opinion should start in a monumentally persuasive way with a slogan of some sort, like Martin Luther King with "I have a dream…" or Winston Churchill with "We shall never surrender." In real life, however, there are many protocols that speakers follow that help open and close their speeches - ones that even Martin Luther King and Churchill used.

Sample task

'Students in secondary school leave with no idea about work. Schools should do more to allow their students to seek part-time work or to do work placements.'

Write a speech to deliver to Year 11 students in assembly in which you explain your point of view on this statement.

How to improve your answer

Writing openings can be difficult, especially if you think that speeches should start in a dramatic way. The reality is that most speakers start by thanking the host of the event where they are speaking. Speeches are often slow and build up momentum. Like letters, there's no reason to be impolite, rude, harsh, critical, angry or aggressive in tone, even if you hold very strong opinions.

Let's start with some introductions that are real turn-offs.

My name is Philip Pirrip and I am a Year 11 student. I'm here today to talk to you about...

Are you even still awake?

That's not to say you shouldn't introduce yourself, but just a reminder that you might want to avoid doing it in the same way that many others will be.

You also might want to avoid another very popular approach that has lost a lot of its power: the rhetorical question, or the question you then answer.

Are you interested in a part-time job?

I am.

Have ever considered getting a part-time job?

I have.

So how can you start instead? Many speakers start by briefly thanking the host and asking for the audience's attention. They refer to the context of the speech and the event at which the speech is delivered.

Thank you, Mr Scruton, for giving me an opportunity to speak to you all today about a topic that is very important to me: the world of work. I know that's probably not the most exciting topic for you, and you were probably hoping for someone to stand up today in assembly and share some miracle secrets to help you get through GCSE History...

> Thank you, Mr Scruton, for that very kind introduction and for allowing me to steal the stage for five minutes of our assembly to share my thoughts with you about …

Another thing that can help you start is explaining who you are and why this topic is important to you. Not all your audience will know who you are. Even if you were doing this speech for real, most of the people in the audience won't know why it's important to you. That's especially true if you are delivering your speech to people beyond the school. Like the letter, you can do this in more gentle ways. You don't need to say it as clearly or robotically as, "My name is Philip Pirrip and I have been at St Arnold's since…" You can also use a bit of humour, especially if you're speaking to your classmates. If it's your classmates, you can do this even if your subject will turn out to be one that is very serious as long as you have a discourse marker like, "But seriously though…"

> Thank you, Mr Scruton, for giving me an opportunity to speak to you all today about a topic that is very important to me: the world of work. I know that's probably not the most exciting topic for you, and you were probably hoping for someone to stand up today and share some miracle secrets to help you get through GCSE History. Most of you probably just think of me as that girl with the strange hair and glasses, always buried in books, too ignorant to even say hello…

> Thank you, Mr Scruton, for that very kind introduction and for allowing me to steal the stage for five minutes to share my thoughts with you about the world we're going to be facing - be that in six

months, three years or ten years. Work! Most of you would be forgiven for thinking I'm not the most forward-thinking year 11 student - especially if you know my reputation for handing in homework late.

If you're faced with a different audience, you can tailor your thanks and your introduction appropriately. Say, for instance, that the task was asking you to address a local forum for business owners instead of your Year 11 classmates.

Thank you, Mrs Howard, for having given me the opportunity to address you this evening. I appreciate that listening to some unknown teenager lecture you about the importance of work experience probably doesn't seem as vital to you as the other items you have on the agenda. I hope, if you give me five minutes, that I'll be able to change your mind on that...

And just like a letter, we want to steer clear of the adjectives and the exaggerated thanks.

Thank you, Mrs Howard, for having given me the wonderful opportunity to address you this evening. I'm very grateful to have five minutes of your very valuable time and I know that you have other much more important issues to deal with this evening. I promise to be as quick as possible...

Your goal is to be polite and to explain that your audience may not share your passion - yet! - but that you hope to change their mind on that, at least a little. Don't set it up to sound like you're apologising for wasting their time or that your topic is not important. Speak as if you have a right to.

You can then start your speech in proper. You can start perhaps with their assumptions, put yourself in their shoes, perhaps ask a question or two. Whilst letters have that lovely way of ending in very formal and fairly familiar ways, speeches can be harder to end. One way to end is to go back to some of the techniques you used for your article and your letter: write **a conclusion** that weaves your ideas together, **summarise** your main point or **leave with a call to action**.

Work experience, as you can see, is so much more than just...

Hopefully you now know why I think work experience is such a vital...

With all this in mind, I'm sure you now understand...

You can also give them something to think about, or finish with a rhetorical question.

All I have left to ask is; where will you go for your work experience?

So with all that in mind, all that remains to ask is...

When you think of yourself ten years in the future, what do you see yourself doing? What career lights your fire? What ways can you imagine to make money that sets your soul on fire rather than leaving you with that sinking Monday morning feeling?

You may not have thought about the future all that much, but perhaps, over the next day or so, spend a little time day-dreaming, a little time imagining...

Remember to thank them for listening to you!

~ Development, structure and organisation ~

Another aspect of writing to focus on is the way you structure, link and develop your ideas in all types of writing.

At GCSE, basic answers might have one or two simple, linked ideas. Many students will then go on to use a variety of ways to develop their ideas and link them. The most skilled and successful responses will use subtle and creative ways to link their ideas across the whole passage.

How to improve your answer

Good plans help build up to a twist or a turning point. They also help you work out how much is possible in the short time available. A plan is essential to help you work out what is manageable and where you are going to end up. Spider diagrams or mind maps can be helpful when you're trying to generate ideas, but they are not at all helpful to help you organise them.

Narrative or chronological writing is easier to plan than many other types. That said, many stories still end unexpectedly or unpredictably. They introduce ideas that have not been planned. Characters are introduced but have no purpose. Sometimes, students write themselves into a dead end. They have no option other than to rely on 'And then I woke up' or other unrealistic endings. Often there's also no link between the opening and the ending. A plan helps avoid this.

For many descriptions, a plan helps you to be detailed and developed, as well as giving your writing a sense of direction. It can help you generate ideas so that you don't run out of content.

In non-narrative writing such as articles, letters or speeches, a plan is essential. Because there may be no logical sequence or order, it's vital that you do things to lock those ideas into a sequence. A reader should not be able to take your paragraphs and rearrange them in another way. Organising non-narrative writing is tough because there's no natural order to it.

Planning is vital for all types of writing.

Your plan should help you account for what is manageable in 45 minutes?

- A short narrative with one or two central characters and a single event or moment.
- A clear description over four or five paragraphs.
- A short essay, article, speech or letter with three or four clearly developed ideas, sandwiched between an introduction or conclusion.

So what plans can help?

A narrative plan is actually fairly easy:

Beginning

Middle

End

If you're crafty, you'll include some of the structural devices discussed earlier when exploring the structure of reading passages. Go back to the section on structure to remember all the techniques you could think of using. Some simple techniques might be things like flashbacks, cliffhanger and turning points.

You also need a fairly simple story structure with a limited number of characters. Two or possibly three maximum. You need to focus on a single event. Things that work particularly well tend to be things with a twist, where the reader learns something unexpected about one of the characters.

For this, you can start with a character. Use stereotypes to your advantage.

For example, a headteacher.

What do we think about headteachers? They are polite, law-abiding, upstanding members of the community.

So a story here would have a twist that the headteacher was not law-abiding.

Work from the ending. What is your final revelation?

The ending: the headteacher painted some graffiti on the school wall and drove off having had enough. She's going to have painted 'I hate this school!' on the wall and walk off.

But if the story starts with her spray-painting a wall, the reader will know from the beginning. So the ideal starting point is making the reader think that she's just there to clean it up. That it's just another day at school.

In the middle, there could be a scene with some teachers and some students. It would be really clever if the students are either really polite - going against the stereotype we'd have in this story - or set up to sound as if they are the type of students who would paint graffiti on a wall.

So the story meets the basic requirements. One major character. One scene. A revelation.

By planning backwards, the writer can put in a flashback paragraph just before the end to show the headteacher painting the graffiti. They might also have a circular structure, including some details from the beginning in the ending. They could plan in some foreshadowing and pathetic fallacy with the weather: heavy rain clouds at the beginning that break at the end.

Planning these rather than expecting them to happen accidentally as you are writing is the best way to go about this.

So, you need:

- A simple cast of characters.
- To plan backward from the revelation at the end.
- To build in a structural device or two, such as a flashback or a flashforwards, or switching between external actions and internal thoughts.

It doesn't need to be anything complicated.

Other things that you can take into account for a narrative plan are the three main components of narrative: action, description and dialogue.

You can decide where you're going to put these before you write to slow the reader down, to speed them up again, to add some pace.

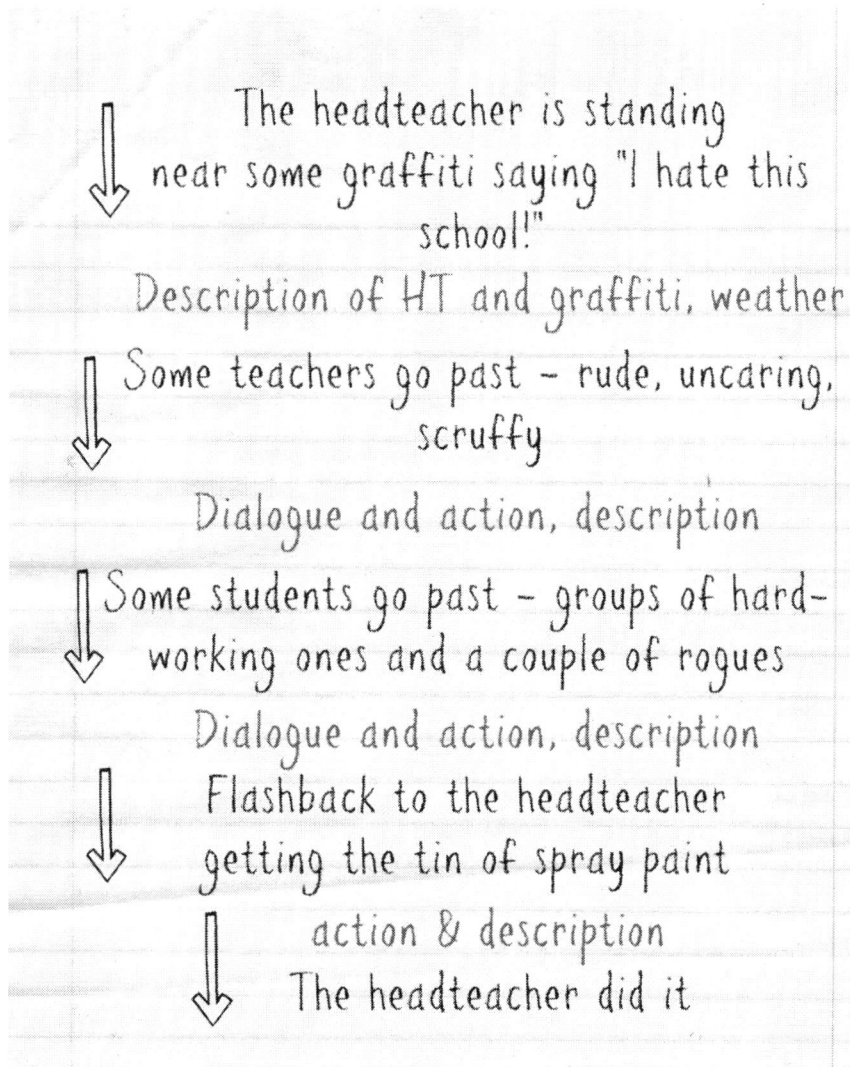

The headteacher is standing near some graffiti saying "I hate this school!"
Description of HT and graffiti, weather
Some teachers go past - rude, uncaring, scruffy
Dialogue and action, description
Some students go past - groups of hard-working ones and a couple of rogues
Dialogue and action, description
Flashback to the headteacher getting the tin of spray paint
action & description
The headteacher did it

Description works differently from narrative, although you could use a linear plan like the one above. However, if you plan like this, the risk of you focusing more on the story of the piece is quite significant.

Some students use plans using the five senses for description. This is not particularly helpful or natural, leading to some poor choices. The problem is that description is non-linear and non-narrative. That makes it a tougher choice in some ways.

One of the easiest ways to plan a descriptive piece is to imagine 360° around, using place prepositions. Place prepositions go from the simple *in, on* or *up* to the divine *beside, between,* and *beyond.*

Start by imagining yourself in the scene.

yet further still

between   above   at the top

behind   Me   beneath

beyond   in the distance

below

underneath

The prepositions you'll choose will be specific for the scene, so if you were describing a person they would be different than the prepositions you'd choose if you were describing a place. Use the 360° image to imagine all sides, up and down, behind and in front, to help you visualise what it is you're trying to describe.

Once you've added your prepositions, add your nouns. Here, you're going to add what you can see and hear, possibly a smell if it helps create the scene. You do not need to add touch or taste unless they would naturally be things you wanted to write about.

After this, plan in some adjectives. What doesn't work are forced, unnatural adjectives for every single noun. So if you were planning a response about a frightening place, and you had planned to write about a scary castle with turrets, a window, the door, sticking two adjectives on every single noun will make your writing sound very clumsy and artificial: the grey, pointed turrets; the empty, broken window; the huge, wooden door. While two adjectives can be very effective in places, they are not effective if you do them all the time.

Once you've added some adjectives, think about where you might want to put some figurative language. Plan in your similes and metaphors.

Finally, decide which connect together. It makes no sense to go from the turret to the kitchen to the door to the stables to the window. What is helpful is to think in terms of a 'guided tour', as if you are showing someone around. What also helps is to think of the place at two different times of day or two different time periods and to include a pivot point. For instance, in describing the castle as empty and derelict, a turning point such as "It wasn't always like this" allows you to move back and describe the scene at another point in time. That gives you not only more content but the ability to mirror your ideas.

So, you need:

- Some notes on what you are going to describe

- To think about the order of those things.

A good plan will help you organise your ideas in a logical way and make choices so that the reader can see that logic. Even in descriptive writing, you might be revisiting details you had at the beginning of the passage and coming back to them at the end.

Organising non-narrative writing need not be too complicated. Where you are constructing an argument of sorts (or at least trying to express your viewpoint coherently), not planning what you write can make your argument really weak. You come up with the most important reason half way through. You forget other reasons. You spend too long on one or another.

A good plan needn't be long. It simply takes a handful of ideas you've come up with and puts them into order so that they are logical.

If you have followed the advice above about articles, letters and speeches, that should help you make connections from the beginning to the end. A summary paragraph is a good way to bring all your ideas together and bring everything to a conclusion.

You could use:

- Connections from the opening to the ending.

- Linked ideas and vocabulary between one paragraph to the next.

- Discourse markers (words that link your ideas and signal a change, addition, consequence or summary for example).

- Linked ideas and vocabulary between one sentence and the next within a paragraph.

Let's have a look at some ideas for an essay. The student had to write an essay about work experience. They wanted to say that work experience was not useful and should be abandoned. To generate ideas, they put themselves into the shoes of people who'd argue the other side - why would they think work experience was useful?

For this, they just used a simple table and a list of ideas as they came into their head:

Reasons why people would say we should do work experience	Counter-arguments
It helps you prepare for the real world	It doesn't - because you're just doing menial tasks
It gives you a sense of the value of work	Most of the time you don't get to see the reality of the work
It helps you pick out jobs	It might provide you with opportunities and contacts when you're 21, but not when you're 15.
It helps you decide if a job is right for you	Work is often a lot less fun than school - and that is not a motivation!
It might give you a way in to a certain career and provide you with contacts	
It helps you identify what you need to do to get that job, what skills you need	
It might give you an opportunity	
School is nothing like work and you can't learn about work in a classroom	

All they do next is start working through the counter arguments and think of ways to argue against those ideas.

Once you have between three to five ideas, you can then consider their order.

Here are four of the counter-arguments from the sample plan:

- Work experience doesn't give you an insight into the real world because you're just doing menial tasks that are nothing like the real job.
- Most of the time you don't get to see the reality of the work: it's boring, it's dull, it involves things that aren't related to the job you envisaged, like accounts and advertising and meetings.
- It might provide you with opportunities and contacts when you're 21, but not when you're 15.
- Work is often a lot less fun than school - and that is not a motivation!

As they stand at the moment, they're just how they came out. There's no sense of order or importance.

One way to organise them better is to rank them in order of importance. Start with your most important idea and finish with the least important. This way, you get your audience's attention right from the start and deliver a powerful opening. The drawback of this approach is that you then lose power.

1. You're just doing menial work.
2. You don't see the reality of the job.
3. Not an incentive!
4. It's not useful for contacts.

So you might then decide to finish with a bang. Lots of politicians do this and you'll find it in lots of speeches where they build up to a powerful crescendo.

The good thing about doing this is that it leaves your reader or audience with a very powerful impression. The drawback is that you may never grab their attention in the first place if you start with your weakest ideas.

But you can't have ideas of equal weight. There will be some that are more powerful than others. So that leaves you having to decide where to put those weakest ideas. The best place to put them, then, is in the middle or even remove them. For instance, the idea about making contacts and opportunity doesn't really fit in with the other three, so we could remove it completely.

That will mean that we then have to develop the other ideas a little more fully. But at least there are three well-connected ideas.

Another way to order your ideas is just to follow the natural links.

Because you just do menial work and because you never see the reality of the job (good or bad), it is not an incentive for you to work harder at school.

Once you have decided on a simple order, you are much better placed to start writing. A plan may be nothing more than this:

Because you just do menial work (1)

and because you never see the reality of the job (good or bad), (2)

it is not an incentive for you to work harder at school. (3)

So when we come to write our introduction, we are better placed to write an overview sentence that we then develop in full in the rest of our writing. Nothing is more impressive than being able to look back at the opening paragraph and seeing that the writer has then expanded on that one simple overview, teasing each idea out into three full sections before tying it back together at the end. It shows discipline. It shows forethought. And, most importantly for you in the exam, it shows an ability to organise your ideas.

A key aspect of your writing that your teachers will be looking at is how far ideas carry on throughout the essay. Does the student introduce something new half way through? Or do they stay on track? Staying on track is a crucial part of your ideas. Also, ideas should be difficult to rearrange. A reader should not be able to look at one paragraph and realise it could go just about anywhere else in the essay.

~ Expanding your ideas ~

Expanding your ideas in narrative writing is fairly straightforward. Adding detail, zooming in, adding dialogue or description or switching between an external viewpoint and an internal viewpoint can help you build on your basic plot.

If you have a detailed plan for your descriptive writing, you should also find it less complicated to expand your ideas.

Where students struggle to develop the points that they have to make is often in non-narrative writing. This is true of narrative and descriptive writing as well.

How to improve your answer

Many less successful essays have lots of **tabloid paragraphs**. These are paragraphs that are short and undeveloped. Often they only have one idea and one sentence. Sometimes they are nothing more than a topic sentence, perhaps with a little development. To write successfully, you will need to show you have **a range of developed, connected ideas**. This means you have to extend your little idea into a big idea.

Work experience is pointless because we just end up doing menial tasks, like washing up or sorting out filing. We're not even allowed to answer the phone!

I, for instance, would like to be a dentist. I went on work experience in a dentist surgery and I didn't even get to see inside anyone's mouth.

Also, dentists have to do a lot of other things but we don't get to see that. Some of them go to do presentations and work with other dentists, but I was stuck in a filing cupboard.

This kind of work experience isn't going to make me want to be a dentist. Instead, it's going to put me off. Why would I work hard in school if that's all I've got to look forward to?

As you can see from this example, the student has a range of ideas, but they are not developed or extended.

So how can these be turned into something bigger?

Some students try to add **statistics**.

I, for instance, would like to be a dentist. I went on work experience in a dentist surgery and I didn't even get to see inside anyone's mouth. 96.7% of work experience students said in a survey that they didn't get to do any single part of their ideal career when they were on work experience.

Others try to add made-up **quotes from experts**.

This kind of work experience isn't going to make me want to be a dentist. Instead, it's going to put me off. Why would I work hard in school if that's all I've got to look forward to? Professor Emma Applegate from Lancaster University says: "Most students find work experience very demotivating."

Others try to put in some **rhetorical questions**.

Work experience is pointless because we just end up doing menial tasks, like washing up or sorting out filing. We're not even allowed to answer the phone! Have you ever been stuck in a filing cupboard for 8 solid hours trying to sort out a dentist's paperwork? I have.

The problem with these kind of methods is that they don't sound convincing or authentic: two key words you're aiming to be in your writing. Real writing doesn't have these kind of fake statistics, made-up experts or bizarre rhetorical questions stuck in for the sake of it. Make sure that if you use these techniques to expand your paragraphs that you try to make them sound authentic.

There are other techniques you can also use. Since you are asked in these types of question to explain your opinion, you can start with **explanation**.

Work experience is pointless because we just end up doing menial tasks, like washing up or sorting out filing. It's not real work experience if you're just behaving like a dogsbody and doing all the things that nobody else wants to do, or things that they'd normally do as part of their own work. We may very well be getting an experience of what work is like, but if you want to be a teacher and you apply for work experience in a school, you're not learning about teaching if you're stuck in the science lab cleaning out beakers or helping the librarian categorise books.

In this answer, the student is explaining why this doesn't constitute work experience. Since this is the focus of your essay, the majority of your writing will be made up of explanation. You can see this student is using explanation words (because, since, as, though) and hypothetical language (modal verbs, if).

You can also **give examples**. You can see the student above uses them to help explain what they mean. You don't have to give them as statements: they can also be questions.

We may very well be getting an experience of what work is like, but if you want to be a teacher and you apply for work experience in a school, you're not learning about teaching if you're stuck in the science lab cleaning out beakers or helping the librarian categorise books. If you're in a hairdresser's for your work experience, and all you're doing is sweeping up hair and putting towels in the washing machine, it's not teaching you what being a hair stylist is really about, is it?

Practical examples help your reader really imagine what it is you are saying. They turn it into something physical and concrete they can imagine.

One type of example you may want to use is the **anecdote**: a personal story. It may be personal to you, or to another person.

If you're in a hairdresser's for your work experience, and all you're doing is sweeping up hair and putting towels in the washing machine, it's not teaching you what being a hair stylist is really about, is it? I spent an entire week with a landscape gardener and all I was allowed to do was clean out plant pots. One of my friends went to work with her accountant mother, and she was asked to clean the grime off all the computer cables. Work experience like this doesn't even qualify as real work experience.

Hypotheticals, **imagining positive scenarios** and **describing worst-case scenarios** can also help you give potential examples. You can also think of scenarios in **different locations** or in **different time periods**. It can be interesting to explain how other people have already found solutions to problems.

I, for instance, would like to be a dentist. What I'd imagined doing was perhaps shadowing a dentist or dental nurse, for them to explain what they were doing, perhaps talk about their regular work, to spend a little time with me going through a patient treatment plan. You can imagine how disappointed I was to find myself sitting at a computer in a dark closet on my own, taking records from the 1970s and putting them into their new computer system. Of course, teenagers of the past did not have to think of such things. You just picked up your pliers and your hand-drill, set yourself up in business and wreaked havoc with your clients' teeth. Apprenticeships definitely helped the early dentists get it right.

At the end of each paragraph, it's a good idea to **bring your ideas back round to the opening** again.

... taking records from the 1970s and putting them into their new computer system. Perhaps I was a little naive to think that I would be allowed to observe, but my experience certainly taught me little about dentistry. Work experience for me was a complete washout and I'd have been better to have stayed in school for the week catching up on revision.

You can also use this circular technique in narrative or descriptive writing. A good way to do this is to think about the links between the opening and the ending. Before you write your final paragraph, check back to your opening paragraph and make sure there are clear links. You can use repeated vocabulary, similar ideas or similar sentence structures. Don't make it too obvious, though, as that doesn't read well.

Let's see how one writer has paused to think before writing her final paragraph. This is the opening paragraph.

Miss Lawley was angry. Really angry. The graffiti said it all: "I hate this school!" Huge, angry letters that ran the length of the sports hall. Clumsy letters. A novice with a spray can. The paint had run, white rivulets that pooled on the asphalt. An inexpert hand. The A was much bigger than the other letters, and the L at the end seemed like it had been painted by a toddler who was running out of paint. Still, the raw sentiment was very clear. The empty spray can lay discarded on the grass and the paint was barely dry. Had it really come to this, she wondered.

Before they write the final paragraph, they look back and pick out some key ideas. Can you see what they've linked to as they finish their story?

That anger and rawness had left her now. She picked up the spray can from the grass and put it in her handbag. Then she reached out a hand and tentatively touched those letters, dry now. I really do hate this school, she thought. Everything about it. The bratty kids, the inept teachers, the stinking ignorance and loneliness that surrounded her. It was a shame it had come to this and she wondered how long it would be before the staff and the pupils realised their headteacher hadn't been seen for days. No doubt they'd think some child had painted this clumsy statement. That was a shame really. Perhaps she should have signed it? A bit late now - she had no paint left.

Miss Lawley smiled without a shred of regret at her angry message, turned on her heels and walked towards the car park for the final time.

Can you see the links? Anger, rawness, the spray can in the grass, the drying letters, the message, the repetition of 'coming to this' and the fact she had run out of paint. Make sure you link your opening and ending using similar devices.

With these techniques to expand your responses, you should find you're more able to develop your ideas in a more convincing way rather than relying on inappropriate rhetorical questions, incongruous statistics and awkward-sounding expert quotes.

~ Technical accuracy:
Sentence structures for effect ~

Technical accuracy is a vital aspect of both narrative and non-narrative writing. Basic responses are made more complicated to read as a result of lack of punctuation or sentence demarcation whereas skilled responses use sentence variety, sentence length, vocabulary and punctuation for very specific effects.

Speeding your writer up and slowing them down, controlling the pace and the tension are things to consider for narrative writing, they're also techniques to use for other writing tasks too. Where short sentences and fragments make a narrative more disjointed, simpler, more tense and more active, in non-fiction writing, these techniques can emphasise your key ideas and underline your main points.

There's no one rule about how many types of sentence there are. There are at least three you should know, and another that isn't technically a sentence but can contribute to the effectiveness of your writing.

What makes a sentence?

Sentences are formed around a verb. That can be a verb phrase or a single verb. Although that is a 'doing' word, it could also be a stative verb, like 'to be' or 'to have'. There are lots of others as well, but sentences form around the verb.

I **switched** on the light.

I **ran** from the monster.

Once we've identified the verb, we can then find the subject: **who** or **what** [verb]?

Who or **what** switched? I switched

Who or **what** ran? I ran

A **simple sentence** is normally formed with one verb and one subject. There are exceptions but by and large, one verb and one subject = simple sentence.

Compound sentences are the next type along. These are formed by two or more simple sentences joined by a FANBOYS coordinating conjunction (for and nor but or yet so), or a comma, or a semicolon.

I switched on the light and a hideous beast jumped out from the corner.

Because the coordinating conjunction 'and' can be replaced by a full stop, and because there are two verbs with two different subjects, this is a compound sentence.

There are some exceptions, but by and large, this rule fits most compound sentences.

A **complex sentence** has a main clause and a subordinate clause which depends on it. There is a main verb and usually one of a number of subordinate conjunctions. These can be for time, place or cause/effect. Sadly, nobody has come up with an effective mnemonic to remember all the subordinating conjunctions and phrases.

After this, we have **sentence fragments**, which are usually without a verb or a subject. Some teachers may also call this a minor sentence.

How to improve your answer

Basic writing depends on simple and compound sentences, or the occasional complex sentence. Writing will often be in sentences that are not demarcated. As writing skills develop, more straightforward responses will have mastered demarcation. This kind of writing will be built mainly around simple and compound sentences, with a few complex sentences that may not be accurately punctuated.

Successful writing at GCSE has a good mix of all three types of sentence, makes varied use of sentence structures and beginning to use fragments for effect.

Skilled writing includes more simple sentences or fragments, as well as sentences for specific effect. These students aren't just thinking 'I've used lots of complex sentences so I'm going to use a sentence fragment for effect', they are thinking this like they want to describe one continuous action and therefore they're going to use a number of linked compound sentences with a number of verbs and no pauses. They also consider how fragments would help add to the disjointed atmosphere here.

Using a range of sentence types and structures is most clear in narrative writing, where they can be used to control the pace. They can also be deployed to great effect in descriptive writing.

A really wonderful example of using sentences for effect in description comes from Charles Dickens' *Bleak House.*

Fog everywhere. Fog up the river, where it flows among green aits and meadows; fog down the river, where it rolls defiled among the tiers of shipping and the waterside pollutions of a great (and dirty) city. Fog on the Essex marshes, fog on the Kentish heights. Fog creeping into the cabooses of collier-brigs; fog lying out on the yards, and hovering in the rigging of great ships; fog drooping on the gunwales of barges and small boats. Fog in the eyes and throats of ancient Greenwich pensioners, wheezing by the firesides of their wards; fog in the stem and bowl of the afternoon pipe of the wrathful skipper, down in his close cabin; fog cruelly pinching the toes and fingers of his shivering little 'prentice boy on deck. Chance people on the bridges peeping over the parapets into a nether sky of fog, with fog all round them, as if they were up in a balloon, and hanging in the misty clouds.

As you can see, it starts with a fragment. *Fog everywhere.* Since there is no verb in it, this is 'less than' a simple sentence. The second 'sentence' is also a fragment as there aren't complete verbs in it:

Fog up the river, where it flows among green aits and meadows; fog down the river, where it rolls defiled among the tiers of shipping and the waterside pollutions of a great (and dirty) city.

What we see with the second sentence is the beginning of a pattern:

Fog up the river, where it flows among green aits and meadows; fog down the river, where it rolls defiled among the tiers of shipping and the waterside pollutions of a great (and dirty) city.

Both start with 'fog' and then a preposition to say where the fog was, 'up' or 'down'. Then we have a comma and a 'where it...' and we're told how it moves and where it goes.

Here, those long sentences drift just like the fog does. Ask yourself: where would you put a full stop? Full stops end things. They divide. They separate. That's not how fog moves. Those long, aimless, verbless, drifting sentences reflect most perfectly how fog moves.

Of course, you don't have to be Dickens to use sentences for effect. Being conscious of why you are using different types of sentences and trying to use them for effect can really help.

- Make sure you use a **range** of sentences appropriately.
- Think what **type** of sentence will work best before you commit yourself to writing it.
- Try to make the idea or the mood of the sentence match the type of sentence you use.

A range of different types of sentence can also be used to help you explain your point of view in non-narrative writing. Some writers use **simple sentences** to make their main point:

Work experience is a waste of time.

They then go on to explain and embellish using **longer sentences** to control the pace and give examples.

Work experience is a waste of time. Many people say it builds useful contacts for your career in the future, and although that might be true if you're doing a work placement when you're just about to start your first job, it's not so useful when you're only fifteen and you've got another five or six years of study in front of you.

Here, the student goes from a short, brief sentence that conveys the main idea simply and then on to a longer sentence to give the reason why.

You can change the pace again and add some variety in the middle of your paragraph to make sure it doesn't get harder to concentrate on your ideas in the middle. Take:

Work experience is a waste of time. Many people say it builds useful contacts for your career in the future, and although that might be true if you're doing a work placement when you're just about to start your first job, it's not so useful when you're only fifteen and you've got another five or six years of study in front of you. In five years' time, who'll even remember you? Nobody. The people who hire and fire could have moved on anyway. Better to spend those two weeks in school focusing on the education you need to get into college, or into university, than to spend two weeks learning how hot your employer likes their coffee made.

Now compare with:

Work experience is a waste of time. Many people say it builds useful contacts for your career in the future, and although that might be true if you're doing a work placement when you're just about to start your first job, it's not so useful when you're only fifteen and you've got another five or six years of study in front of you. In five years' time, it's not even likely that anyone would remember that shy, awestruck teenager who spent two weeks hidden in a dusty cupboard filing paperwork from decades before. Better to spend those two weeks in school focusing on the education you need to get into college, or into university, than to spend two weeks learning how hot your employer likes their coffee made.

A change of pace in the middle of the paragraph can really help keep your reader focused. It just makes it more readable. And you might like to have a **simple summary sentence at the end of the paragraph**, just to drive home your main message.

Work experience is a waste of time. Many people say it builds useful contacts for your career in the future, and although that might be true if you're doing a work placement when you're just about to start your first job, it's not so useful when you're only fifteen and you've got another five or six years of study in front of you. In five years' time, who'll even remember you? Nobody. The people who hire and fire could have moved on anyway. Better to spend those two weeks in school focusing on the education you need to get into college, or into university, than to spend two weeks learning how hot your employer likes their coffee made. Then make your contacts when you're ready to work.

By choosing to use simple sentences and fragments to highlight your main points, it makes them clear and easy to understand. This helps make your writing convincing and compelling.

~ Technical accuracy:
Punctuation for effect ~

When your teacher marks your work, they are checking to see if there is a range of punctuation that is appropriate for the writing and whether the punctuation is used accurately.

How to improve your answer

What really helps is having a good understanding about what punctuation does and what is appropriate in narrative or descriptive writing.

   What is really unhelpful is going into your exam, doing a tick list of punctuation at the top of the page and being determined to use them all.

. ! ? " " ( ) - - ... , ; :

What is most common in stories and description?

1. Full stops
2. Commas
3. Speech
4. Apostrophes of omission
5. Apostrophes of possession
6. Hyphens

That is more than enough to be considered to be a range.

What is most common in non-narrative writing?

1. Full stops
2. Commas
3. Question marks

4. Colons

5. Semi-colons

As you can see, full stops and commas are vital in both, but many students still make errors with these. The most common error is using a comma where a full stop should go.

Luckily, speech, apostrophes, question marks, colons and semicolons have very clear rules and can be much easier to master than commas.

Speech and apostrophes are two places many teachers find themselves looking to when assessing how well students understand the rules of punctuation. Because there are clear conventions about the punctuation of speech and the use of apostrophes, they can be a good guide to seeing whether a student has a little understanding for lower grades, or knows the rules for higher grades.

Speech is an excellent way to get in your ? and your ! or your … without relying on checklists and artificial use of lists or unnecessary rhetorical questions in stories. Speech marks would also be useful in non-narrative writing if you were including a quote from someone.

You can see here how a student has used speech marks in narrative writing:

A harried-looking adult was approaching from the car park. Mr Eckers, the Geography teacher. His arms were filled with books and Miss Lawley wondered why he just didn't get a bag. The man was so disorganised. He slowed down as he saw the graffiti.

"Oh dear!" he said, "Oh dear! What's this then?"

Stupid man, Miss Lawley thought. What did it look like? An elephant in custard? He really was infuriating.

"It's graffiti, Mr Eckers." She felt like spelling it out and giving him a definition. G-R-A-F-F-I-T-I. Writings or drawings made on a wall or other surface usually without permission.

"Oh." he said. "Oh dear!"

Here the speech helps the reader get a sense of lots of things such as Miss Lawley's frustration, Mr Eckers' inept and bumbling ways. It moves the story along and adds a bit of pace.

You may be wondering whether or not it is acceptable to use speech in description. So often, a little speech (not to turn it into a story) lifts the description. It's a wonderful way to bring life to it. Dialogue in description works particularly well when you zoom in on one person.

The carnival was in town. There'd been an air of anticipation, of agitation, for days, and a small crowd had gathered along the high street to watch the procession come through. At the front, boys who'd skipped school, their books discarded in shop doorways or abandoned on walls. Behind them, young mothers and their excited toddlers, red-cheeked and caught up in the commotion. One mother, her blonde curls trapped under a multi-coloured, hand-knitted hat, lifted up her daughter to see the first performers approach. She pointed along the road, urging the child to look with her.

"Look, Lily! Clowns!"

But her excitement ended there. The child took one look at the sad, white faces and the drooping, painted mouths, the dishevelled appearance and the huge shoes, concluding that these must indeed be monsters, and promptly burst into a fit of tears.

Focusing on a detail like this can really help you bring a scene to life and make it dynamic, rather than just relying on long, drawn-out sentences and purple prose.

In non-narrative writing, speech can be used to add a quote or an opinion:

Not only that, work experience has a long history when it comes to helping you get a job. "Many of the famous painters and sculptors we know now were unpaid apprentices," explained art history professor, James Nettles, "Michelangelo and Leonardo da Vinci would have done a seven-year apprenticeship with an established artist. They'd spend years copying the master's work, understanding how to work with light and shade, colour palettes and surfaces. They'd also have worked with a range of models as well." Their apprenticeships would also find them sponsors for their own professional life. "It's not very much different than life as an unpaid intern these days," Nettles conceded.

As speech marks are such an easy punctuation mark to include in all types of writing, they're definitely something to brush up on. Since they have clear and given rules, they're also much easier to master than the over-used comma.

Summary

1. Revise your apostrophes for omission and possession.

2. Make sure you have a solid grasp on some of the more regular mistakes like *it's* used instead of *its.*

3. Revise speech marks.

4. Make sure you aren't guilty of splicing sentences together with commas.

5. Check your full stops at the end.

6. Understand the purpose of punctuation and its role: where are the different punctuation types most of use?

Focusing on the quality of your vocabulary, the way you organise your writing, your use of sentence structures and accuracy in punctuation will really give you the edge in the exam.

~ Some final words ~

People say it's impossible to revise English. If you're taking English Literature at the same time, your head will be swimming with all the quotes you need to remember, all the themes you need to understand. You know how to revise English Literature: it's like revising History or Geography or Biology. You memorise stuff.

It can be really hard to know how to revise for GCSE English Language, and doubly hard because you have so many other things to memorise. What you need to remember is that English is a skill: it's not cramming your head full of DAFORESTS and anadiplosis. It's the same as Art or Dance or Music: you get better by practising.

Looking back to my own GCSEs - the very first year GCSEs were launched! - I had no idea what to revise, how to revise or even whether I could revise English. I bought a revision guide and asked another English teacher if I needed to know what metonymy was. I didn't dare ask my own English teacher: just to ask was a damning indictment on the things she had taught us.

No, the English teacher said, I did not need to know what metonymy was.

Though that reassured me my lovely English teacher was doing the right thing after all, it didn't help me know what and how to write.

What really did help me was doing it.

Past papers are your way of detecting the patterns, seeing the mechanics behind the exams. Knowing how it works is not cheating. It is not cutting corners. It is understanding the rules. But it is not enough to have understood the rules. Essay practice under timed conditions is the hidden art of exam writing. That comes down to confidence and to priorities.

To have the confidence to find and discuss all the big ideas in a short amount of time is an art in itself. That's why I'm so keen on the Big Ideas.

Being able to focus in on the key details of a text is the most vital reading skill a student can have.

And you get there through repeated practice.

The other thing to remember is that confidence and focus are personal. For the texts used in this book, I could give you The One Big Idea. But that would be the One Big Idea According To Me.

Practising those skills of homing in on key quotes and discussing the big idea is the fundamental skill of both GCSE English and English Literature. It's all about the evidence.

Writing is a little different. You get better at that the more you do. However, and this is an important however, you need feedback. Without feedback, nothing evolves. Feedback can come in the form of discussion, of sharing on student homework sites, on looking at what your friends are doing and seeing how they approach it.

It's all very well to practise and to practise and to practise. But you need feedback and you need to know so you can see for yourself how other students are getting the marks.

And it needs **you** to take an active part in your learning.

This learning process is called 'shaping'. It means when we have feedback, we get a bit closer, a bit closer, a bit closer. A bit better, a bit better, a bit better. Something has to change or evolve each time, or else we're just doing the same thing over and over, getting into terribly bad habits. Some students fall into that trap. There's no feedback and nothing changes. They get better and better and better at writing exactly the same level of answer.

Targeted practice with some feedback is the best way to move forward. Knowing what it is you are supposed to be doing helps a great deal too.

Very best of luck in your exams.

Jane Hallwood

~ Reading texts ~

Text A

In 2015, television presenter Pamela Taylor travelled around the world to make a series about childhood in different countries. Text A is an extract from her autobiography "Nothing Left to Lose" describing jobs she'd had as a teenager.

1   By the time I was twelve, I got my first job, working a milk round before school. We were up at 5 a.m. to make sure all the milk had gone out, clinging onto the back of a milk float* and racing to catch up if we'd left a couple of pints at the bottom of a long driveway.

5   It's no wonder I found school so exhausting. Next came a Saturday job in a greengrocer's shop when I was thirteen, helping stack up the fruit and vegetables. Between the two jobs, that gave me enough every week to buy a couple of magazines, a couple of music singles or a poster of my favourite bands. When I was

10   sixteen, I started working in a local restaurant and then in a bar at eighteen. Those jobs were much less strenuous, that's for sure.

The milk round wasn't bad work, even though it was an early start. Some mornings were cold, and after the clocks went back in autumn, we started in darkness and finished in darkness. In the

15   summer, though, there were definite benefits to being up early. The early morning twilight and blue skies were beautiful: we'd cross foxes from time to time, caught out by the almost-silent purr of the electric milk float. Most of the birds had caught on to our arrival and would peck the tops off the bottles as soon as we left

20   them on doorsteps to get to the cream, and most of our customers

left out yoghurt pots or jam jars to leave over the bottles to deter the birds. It wasn't unknown to leave a milk bottle though and find yourself accompanied by all kinds of avian assistants. It left me with a deep love of those early summer mornings and even now

25   I'm an early bird rather than a night owl.

I can't say the winters were as joyous. Fingerless gloves gave way to double mittens as the winter drew on, and there were times we'd leave skin on bottles if we forgot our gloves. Early frosts meant slower work: you couldn't run back up driveways or long

30   paths if you wanted to avoid slipping. Slipping when you were carrying bottles was definitely a ticket to the hospital so it'd take us much longer on icy days. We were fearless though and I remember sliding 20 metres to the float and grabbing the back as if I was invincible. I definitely earned my wages on those winter

35   days! Our work wasn't unrewarded though, and we got lots of Christmas tips in the weeks up to Christmas. People left out cards and presents for us. We might never have seen our customers, but we definitely felt appreciated.

Other than John, the milkman, it was a world of adolescents. He

40   stayed mostly in the float driving, and we hung off the back or ran to catch up. There were usually three of us most mornings and we'd spend most of our time chatting. We'd hang out on Friday and Saturday nights too. It turns out deep friendships are forged in those ice-cold winter mornings.

45   The greengrocer's was different altogether: a world of grown-ups and better wages. I got a proper wage packet, not a crumpled up fiver at the end of the week. These were the first adults I really got to know other than family or the parents of friends. Anne and

Margaret were two women who ran the shop like a comedy act
50 and I grew to love their sharp humour and acid tones. They taught
me everything about customer service, about service with a smile,
and how work didn't have to be serious. Everybody had their role
and the shop ran smoothly, except when the boss turned up. He
was always harried and panicked, racing between his three shops.
55 He'd had an earlier start than me on my milk round though, getting
up at two a.m. to go to the wholesalers and pick up all the fresh
produce. Anne and Margaret always soothed him and taught me
everything about keeping bosses sweet. Keeping everything going
smoothly was the best way to keep him on side, and the other
60 shops would give us a phone call to let us know he was on his
way so we could make sure everything looked perfect.
Those first jobs gave me a real appreciation of work and the value
of money. I might get celebrity treatment these days as a TV
presenter, but I'll always be proud of how hard I worked to get
65 where I am.

Glossary

* milk float - an open-sided van powered by electricity used for delivering milk to houses

Text B

In 1815, the British Parliament took evidence about factory conditions in England. Text B is taken from a report in which a factory worker named Elizabeth Ogden describes her life in a mill in Leeds.

1   I'm twenty-three years old and I've been working since I was six. The place I worked was a flax mill in Leeds belonging to Mr Burke. We spun the flax to turn it into linen. I was what they call a little doffer, taking bobbins off the machines and replacing them with new ones. When the spinning frames are full, they stop the

5   machines so we can take the full bobbins off and put empty ones on before they start the machine going again. Often the spindles are still moving so we have to stop them as we can. Some of the other workers have broken their hands or feet stopping the spindles moving. Hands and arms can easily get stuck in the

10   machines and there are some who've lost fingers or broken arms. There's a lot of frames and they run quick, so you are constantly running from one machine to another and you haven't time for anything else. It's very hot work. There's a lot of dust from the flax and most of the children have coughs.

15   Our hours were six in the morning to seven at night, but I worked from five in the morning until nine at night when we were busy, and that was most days. The engine room is the beating heart of the mill, and everything after is a noisy wave of click-clacking machines, pistons, pumps, gears, levers, cogs, spindles, cranks,

20   flywheels, throttles and valves. It never ceases. By five o'clock the factory is in full movement. A wind-fan gives us an infernal fog of

heat and moisture. Everything moves in a constant whirring motion and a stench of fumes hangs in the air. It is often intolerable. There is no time for breakfast or drinking. We do as we

25 can when the machines are running and we are often famished. The factory is a sort of prison-house as once the mill gates are locked, you cannot come or go. We are given forty minutes for our meal at noon. The food is very ordinary and not plentiful. Many of us are half-starved.

30 If we were late or if we were slow, we got the strap*. There is no sitting down. It didn't matter how old or how young you were, if you were a boy or a girl, they gave you the strap if you were slow. Sometimes the overlooker is so angry with us he'll take one of the girls and beat her the full length of the room with a chain or with

35 the strap. Once he stripped a boy, tied him to a pillar and beat him with straps for stopping the machines. We worked in link to tell each other when the overlooker was coming, with a code of signals so that we wouldn't get caught out.

I lived two miles from the mill and we didn't have a clock. We were

40 always frightened of getting the strap or not getting paid, so my mother stayed up some of the night. The coal miners were up at three or four o'clock so when my mother heard them stirring, she got up out of her bed and asked them the time.

Mill work is very hard and a lot of the doffers have bent backs. I

45 was thirteen when my back started bending and it's worse since. Some of the doffers have stays* to keep them straight but my mother died when I was seventeen so we never bought any. After she died, I saved my money and bought myself some stays. I

cannot tell you the pain and weariness but I know most of the

50 doffers have pains like that. Some have crooked knees or weak

ankles too.

I've been living in the poorhouse the last year because I cannot

work. The hardship and cruelty I've known in that mill since I was

54 a girl is too much to carry.

Glossary

* strap - a strip of leather, used in this case for corporal punishment

* stays - a stiff garment with whalebone sewed into the seams to keep the

back straight and improve posture

Text C

This extract is taken from the middle of a short story by HG Wells. The narrator has decided to spend the night in a supposedly haunted room in order to prove there is nothing to be scared of.

1   The door to the red room and the steps up to it were in a shadowy corner. I moved my candle from side to side, in order to see clearly before opening the door and I had a sudden twinge of apprehension. I glanced over my shoulder, and opened the door

5   rather hastily, with my face half turned to the silence of the landing.

I entered, closed the door behind me at once, turned the key I found in the lock, and stood with the candle held up surveying the scene, the great red room of Lorraine Castle in which the

10   young duke had died.

There were other and older stories that clung to the room, back to the half-credible beginning of it all, the tale of a timid wife and the tragic end that came to her husband's jest of frightening her. And looking around that large shadowy room, with its shadowy

15   window bays, its recesses and alcoves, one could well understand the legends that had sprouted in its black corners, its germinating darkness. My candle was a little tongue of flame in its vastness that failed to pierce the opposite end of the room

20   and left an ocean of mystery and suggestion beyond its island of light.

I decided to make a systematic examination of the place. I began to walk about the room, peering round each article of furniture, tucking up the sheets of the bed, and opening its curtains wide. I pulled up the blinds and examined the fastenings of the several

25   windows before closing the shutters, leant forward and looked up the blackness of the wide chimney, and tapped the dark oak panelling for any secret opening.

There were two big mirrors in the room, each with a pair of candles, and on the mantel too, were more candles in china

30   candlesticks. All these I lit one after the other. The fire was laid and I lit it, to keep down any desire to shiver, and when it was burning well, I stood round with my back to it and looked at the room again. I had pulled up an armchair and a table, to form a kind of barricade before me, and on this lay my revolver ready to

35   hand.

The echoing of the stir and crackling of the fire was no sort of comfort to me. The shadow in the corner at the end in particular had an odd suggestion of a lurking, living thing, that comes so easily in silence and solitude.

40   At last, to reassure myself, I walked with a candle into it, and satisfied myself that there was nothing there. I stood that candle upon the floor in the corner, and left it there.

By this time I was in a state of considerable nervous tension, although to my reason there was no cause for the condition. My

45 mind, however, was perfectly clear. I decided that nothing supernatural could happen. The sombre reds and blacks of the room troubled me; even with seven candles the place was dim. The one in the corner flared, and the fire-flickering kept the shadows perpetually shifting and stirring.

50 I remembered the candles I had seen in the passage, and returned with as many as ten. These I put in various knick-knacks of china, lit them and placed them where the shadows were deepest, some on the floor, some in the window recesses, until at last seventeen candles were so arranged that not an inch

55 of the room darkened, but had the direct light of at least one. It occurred to me that when the ghost came, I could warn him not to trip over them.

It was after midnight that the candle in the alcove suddenly went out, and the black shadow sprang back to its place. I did not see

60 the candle go out; I simply turned and saw that the darkness was there.

"By Jove!" said I aloud; "That draught's a strong one!" and taking the matches from the table, I walked across the room in a leisurely manner to relight the corner again.

My first match would not strike, and as I succeeded with the

65 second, something seemed to blink on the wall before me.

I turned my head involuntarily, and saw that the two candles on the little table by the fireplace were extinguished.

I rose at once to my feet.

"Odd!" I said. "Did I do that myself?"

70 I walked back, relit one, and as I did so, I saw the candle in the right sconce of one of the mirrors wink and go right out, and almost immediately its companion followed it.

There was no mistake about it. The flame vanished, as if the wicks had been suddenly nipped between a finger and thumb,
75 leaving the wick neither glowing nor smoking, but black.

Printed in Great Britain
by Amazon